Magic,Myth & Monsters:
A Fantasy Coloring book

Issue #1
Created by Steven Fenczik

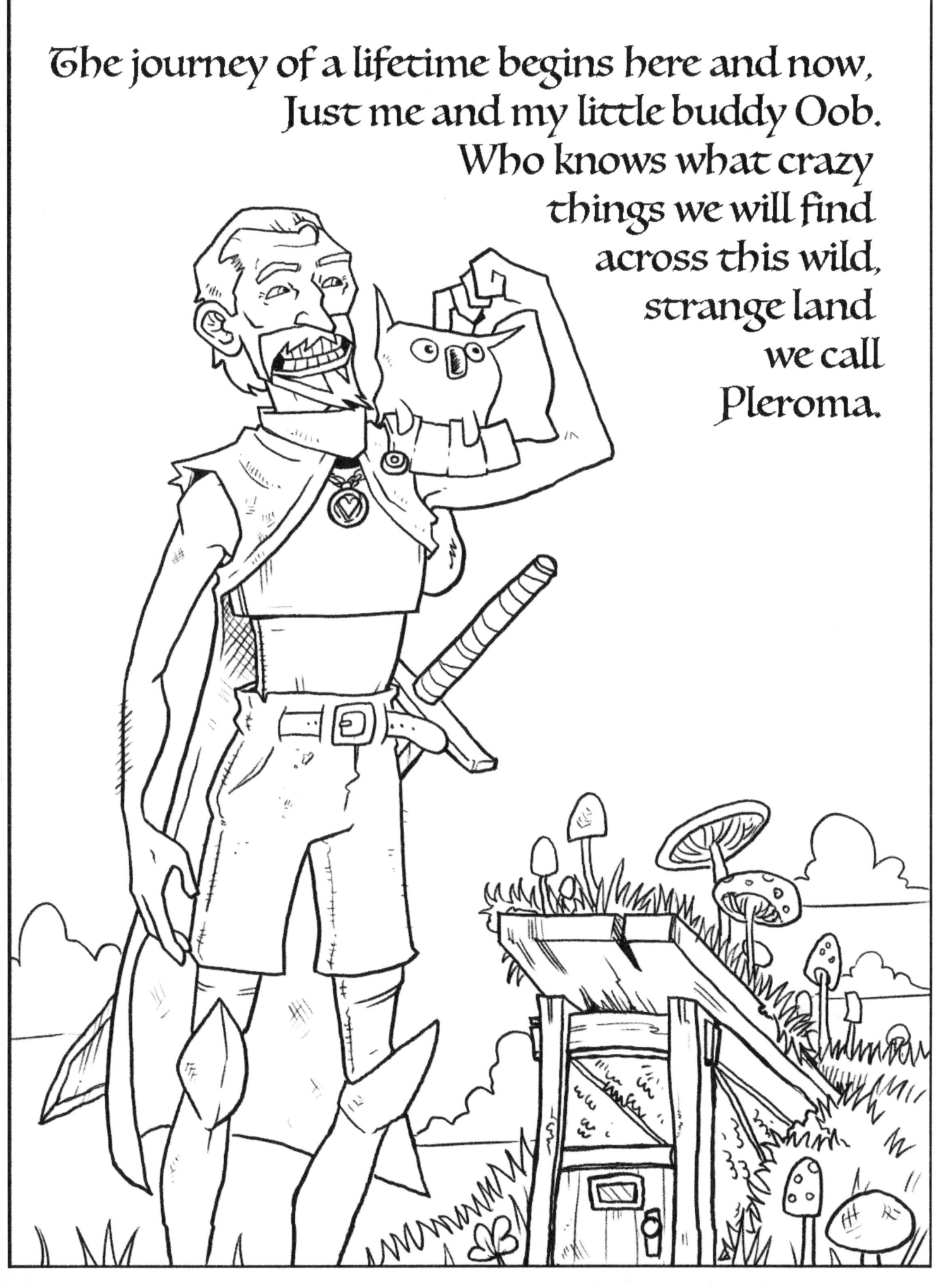

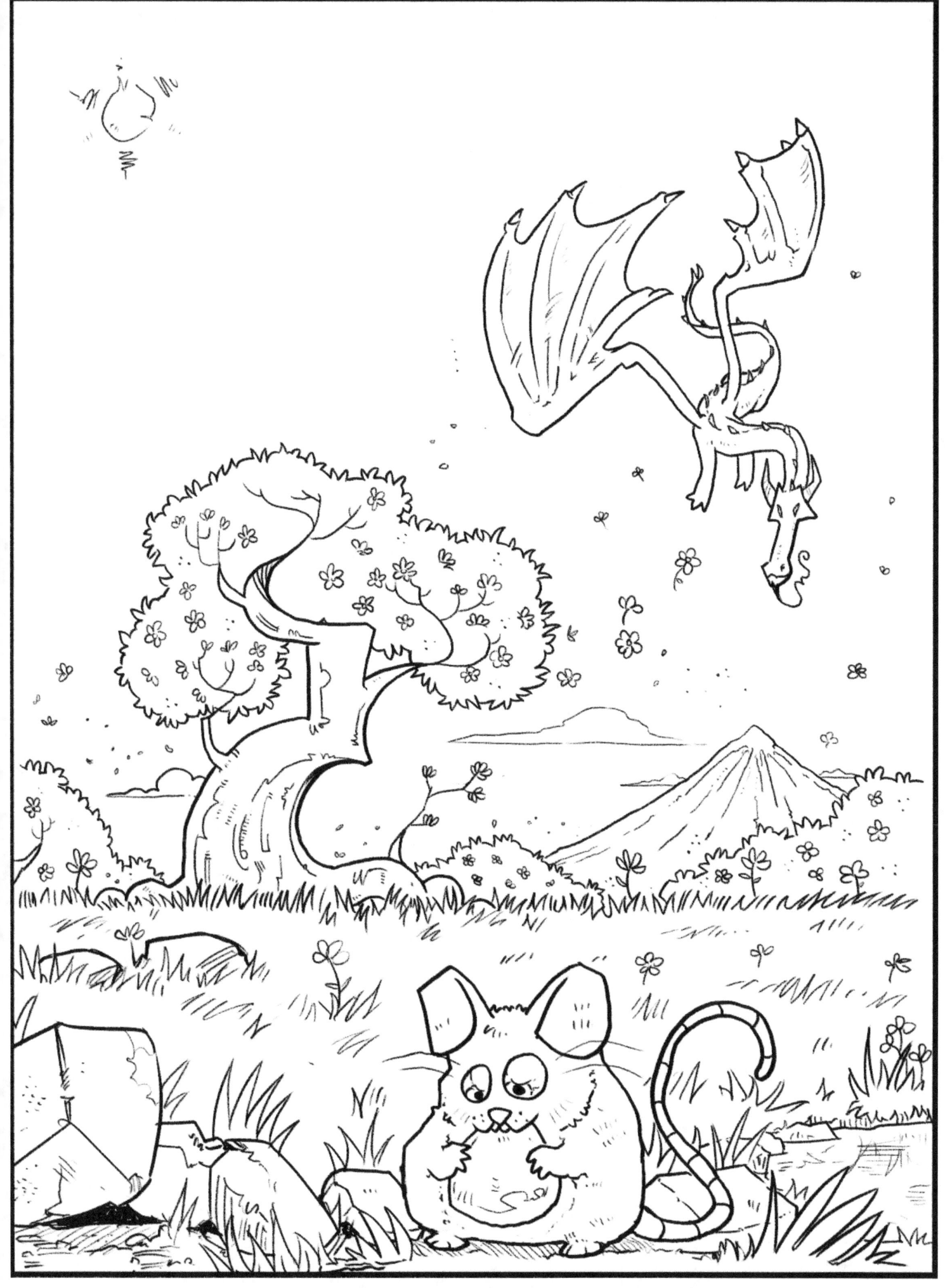

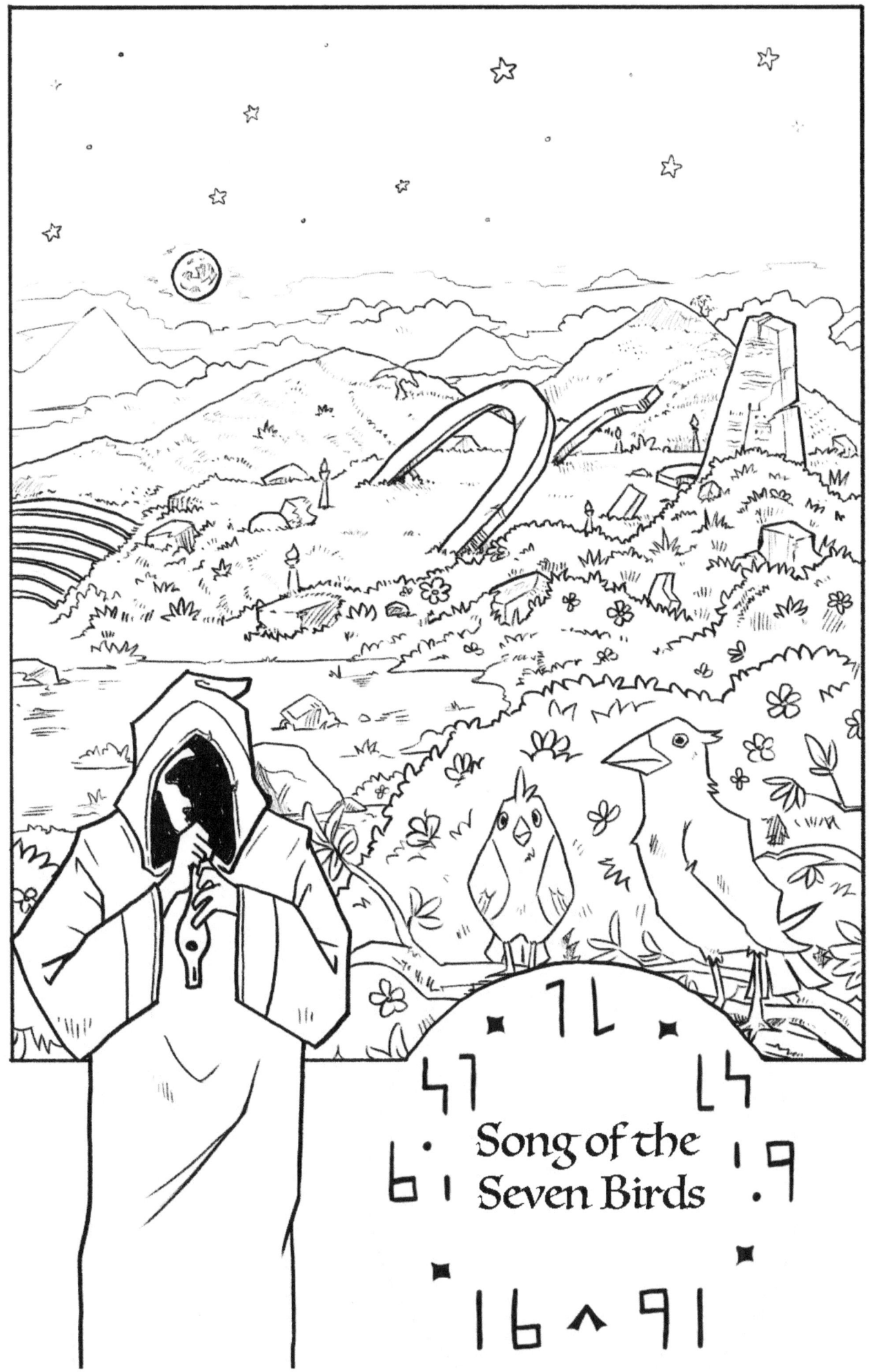

Song of the
Seven Birds

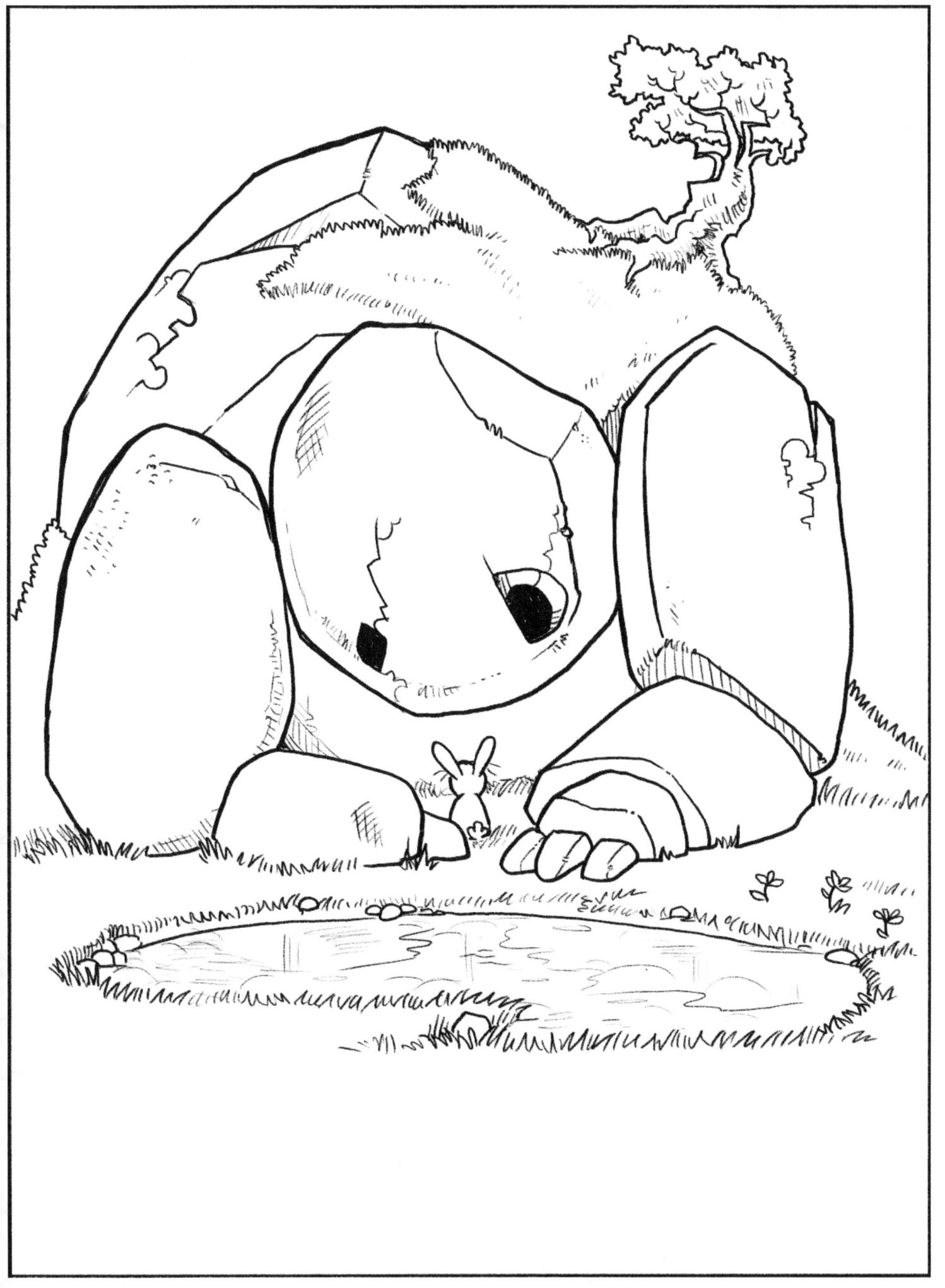

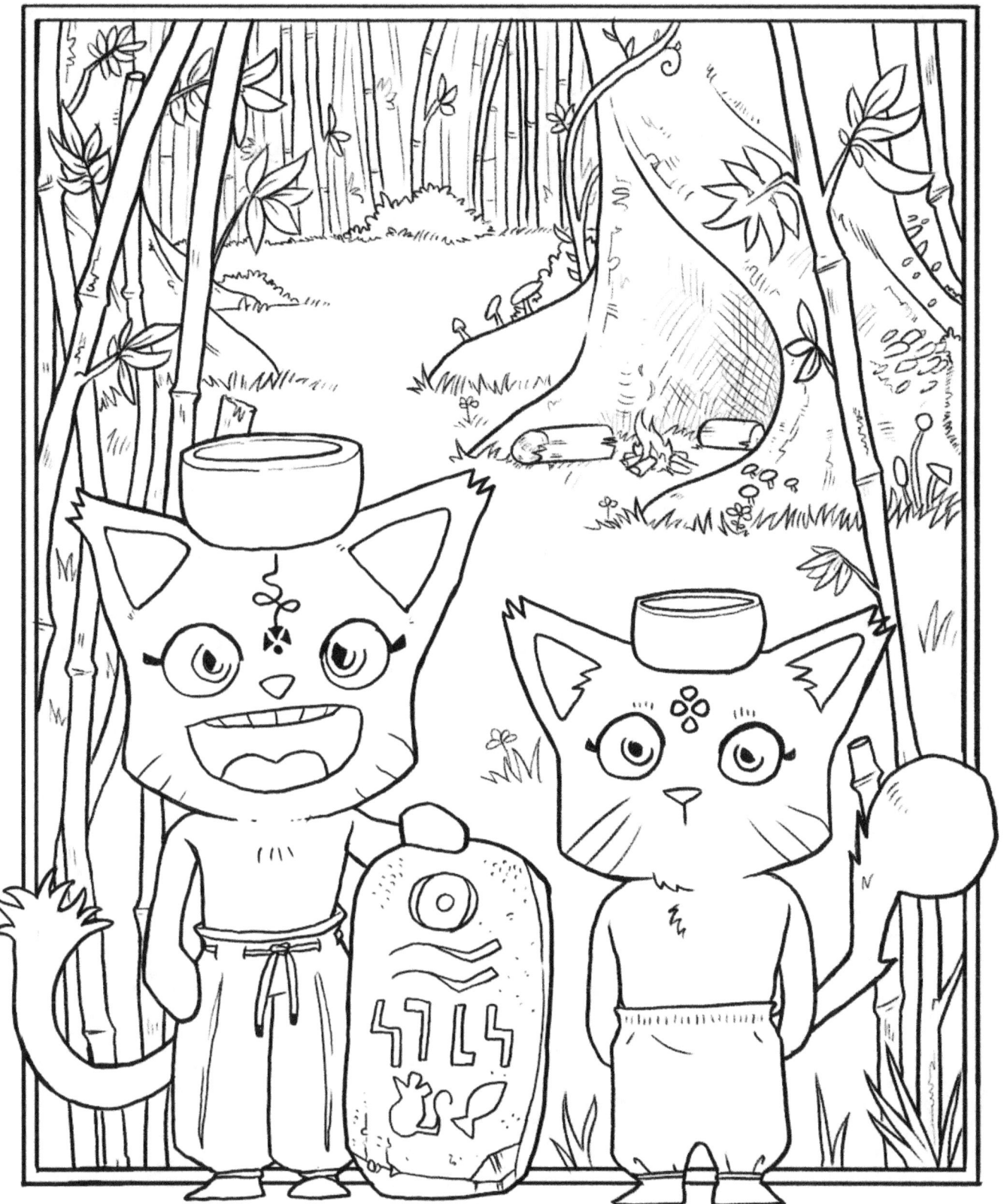

These are the Ascetic Felines of the Bamboo Thicket. Give them Alms and the gods will be pleased.

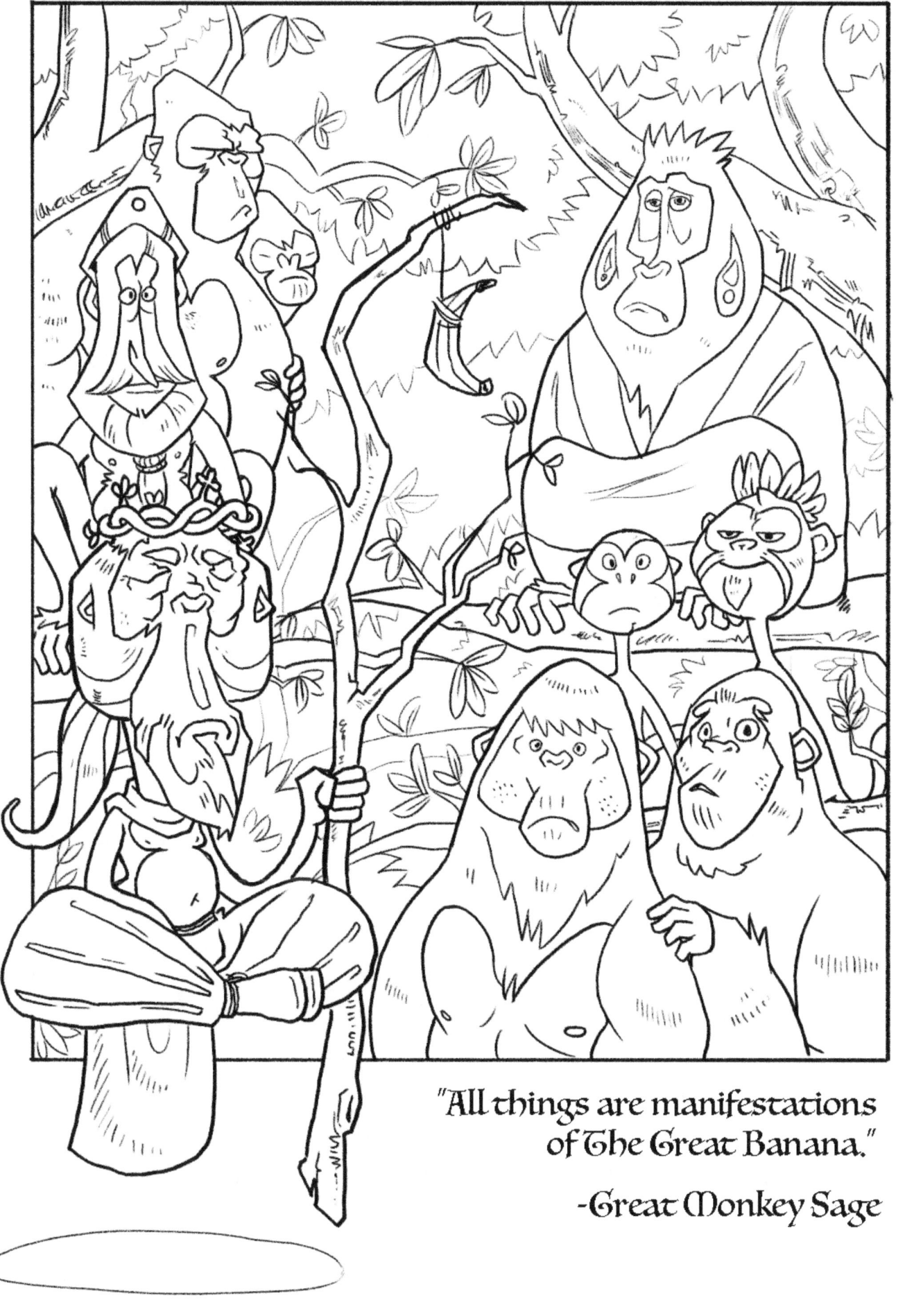

"All things are manifestations of The Great Banana."

-Great Monkey Sage

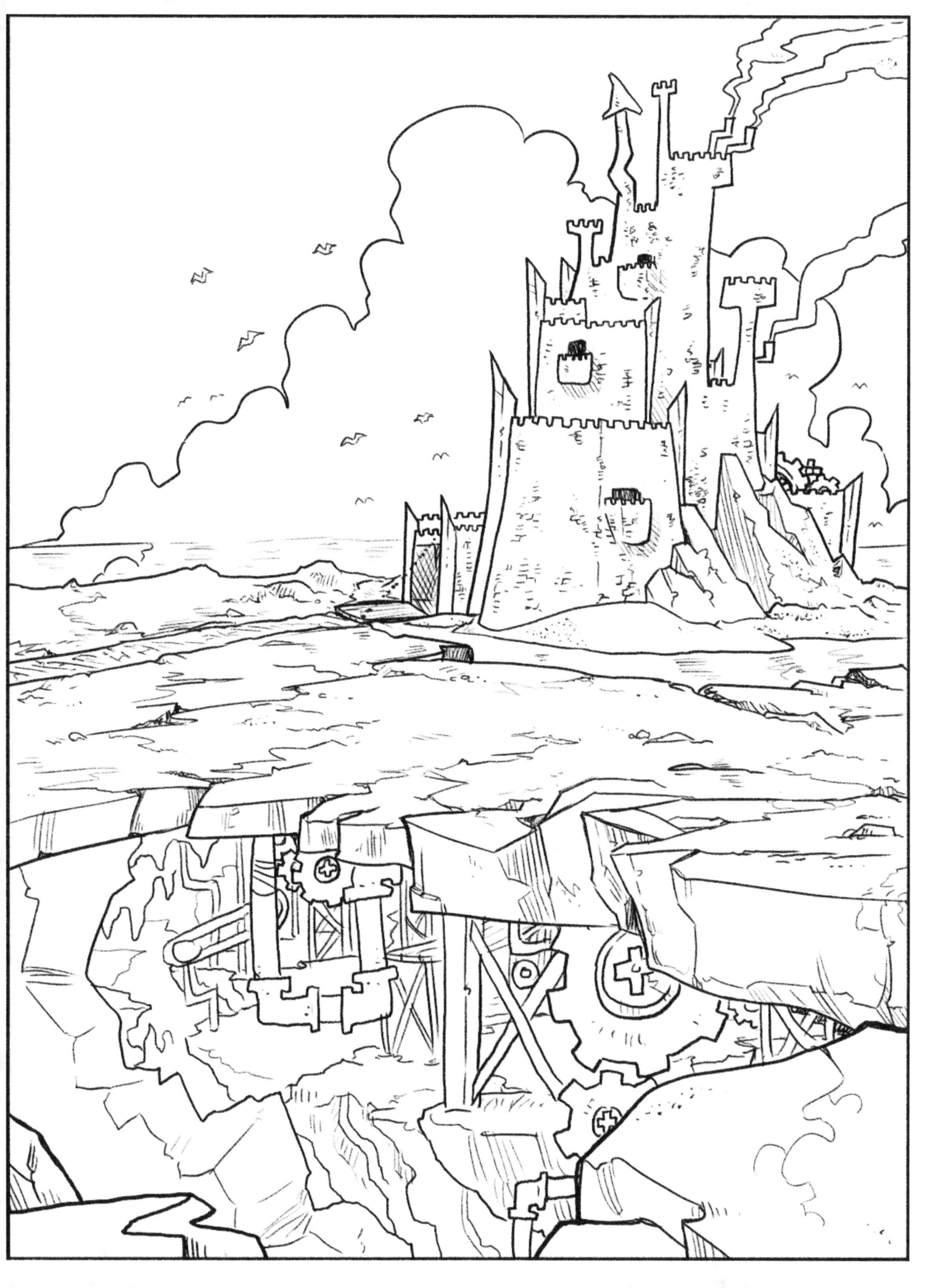

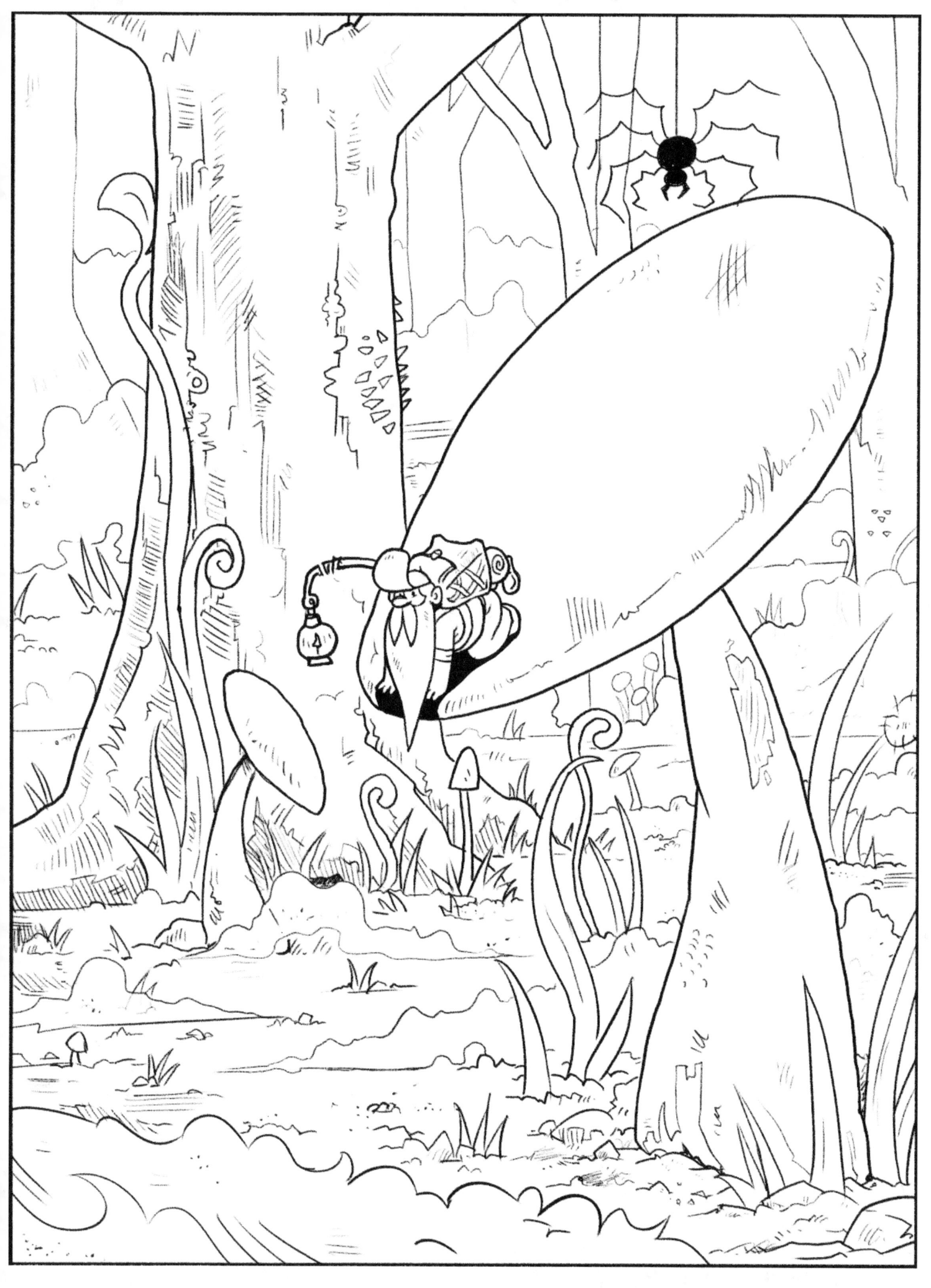

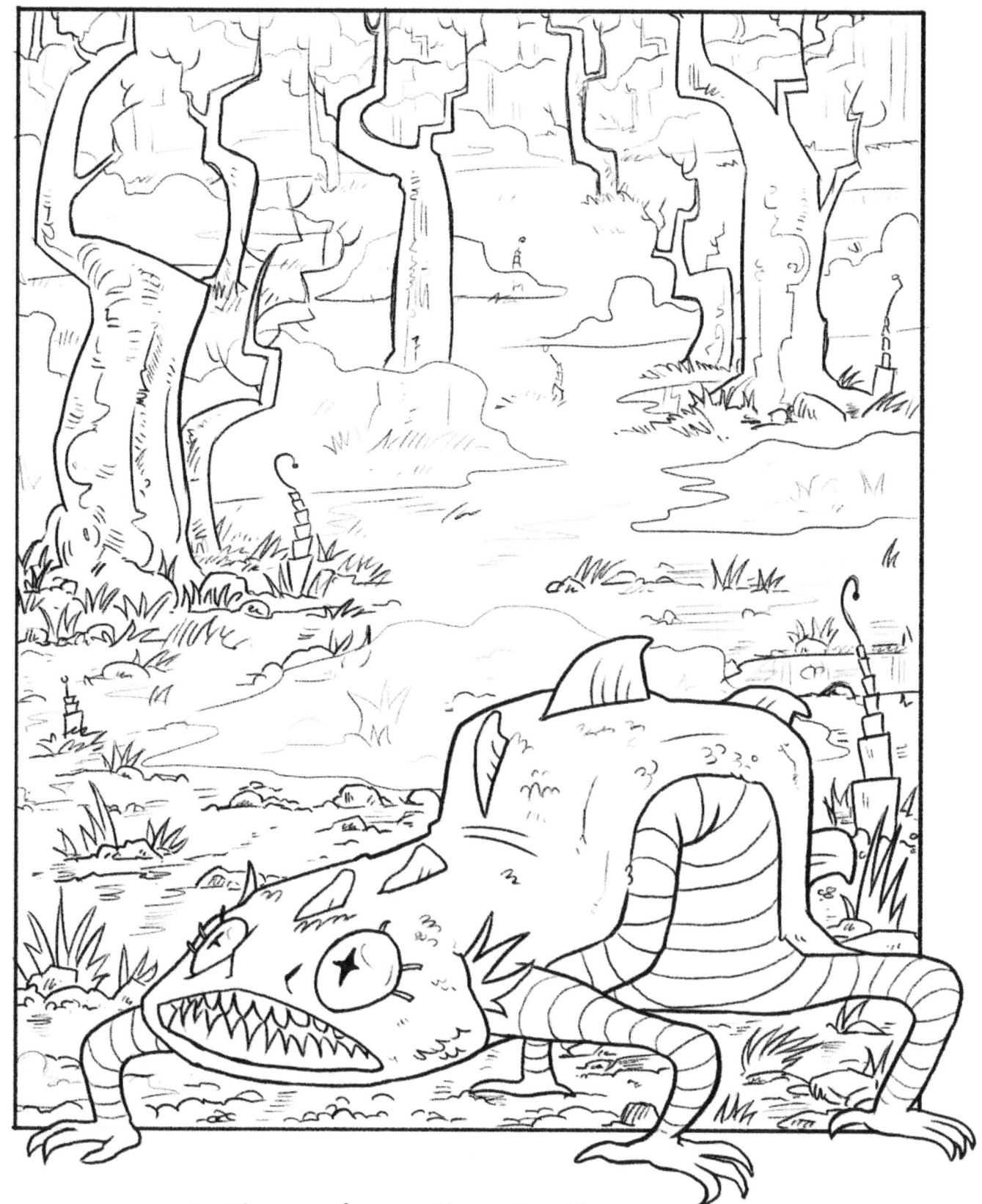

The Crooked Skeez of
The Twisted Marsh has a
poison gleek that could kill 50 men.

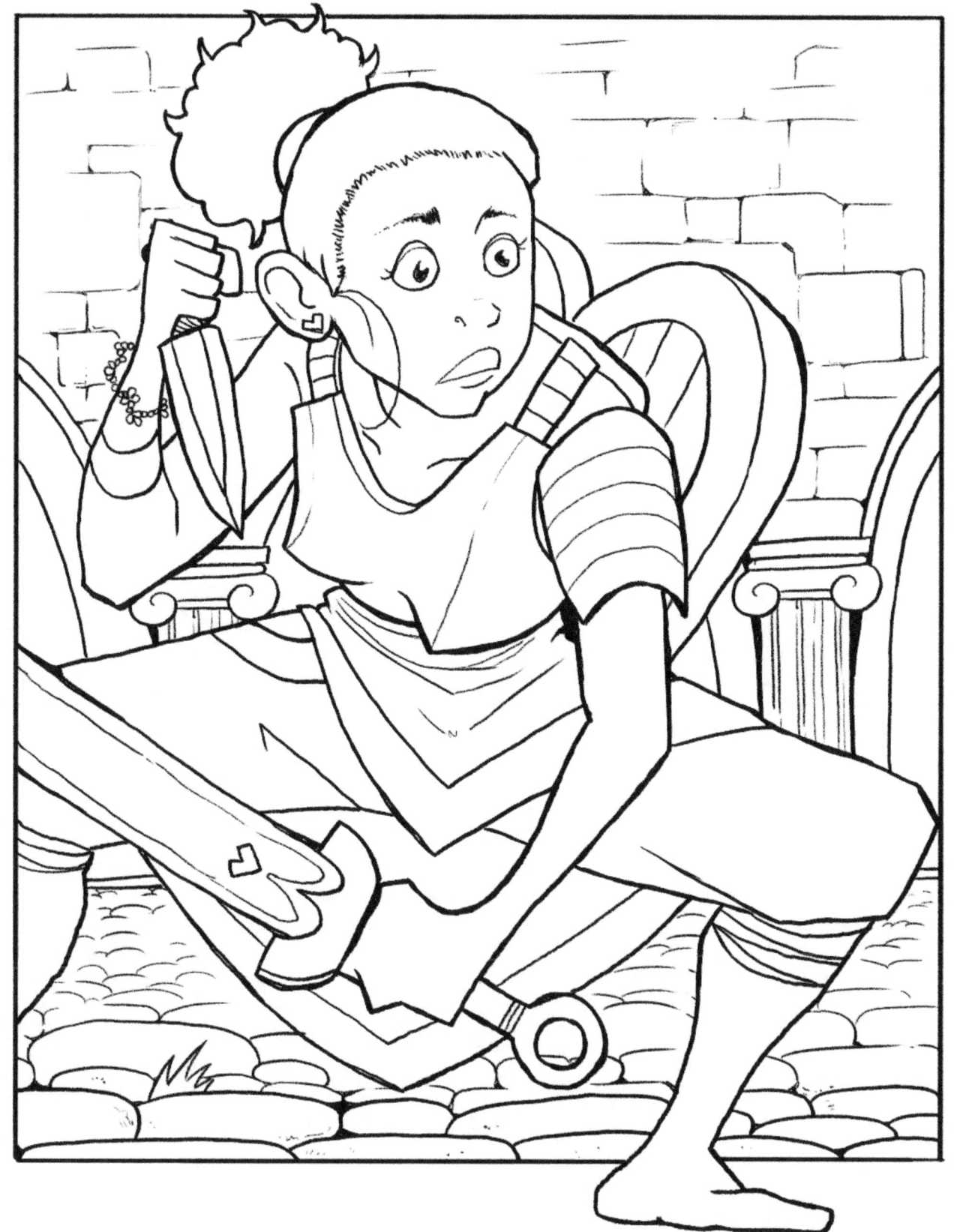

Szara hunts for the stolen heart of
the rain spirit to save her village.

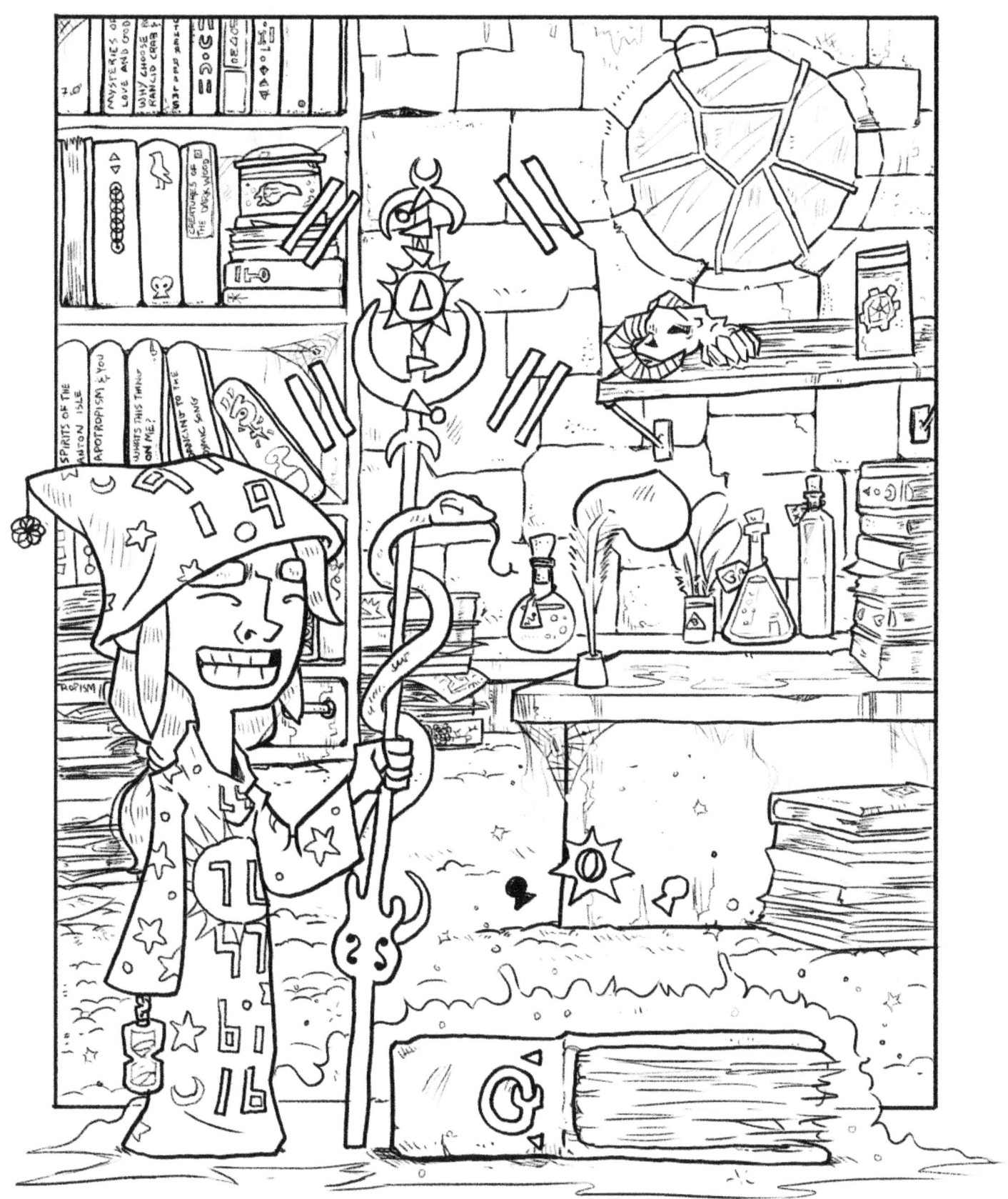

Spells, Talismans, Relics
and Incantations 50% off.
(while supplies last)

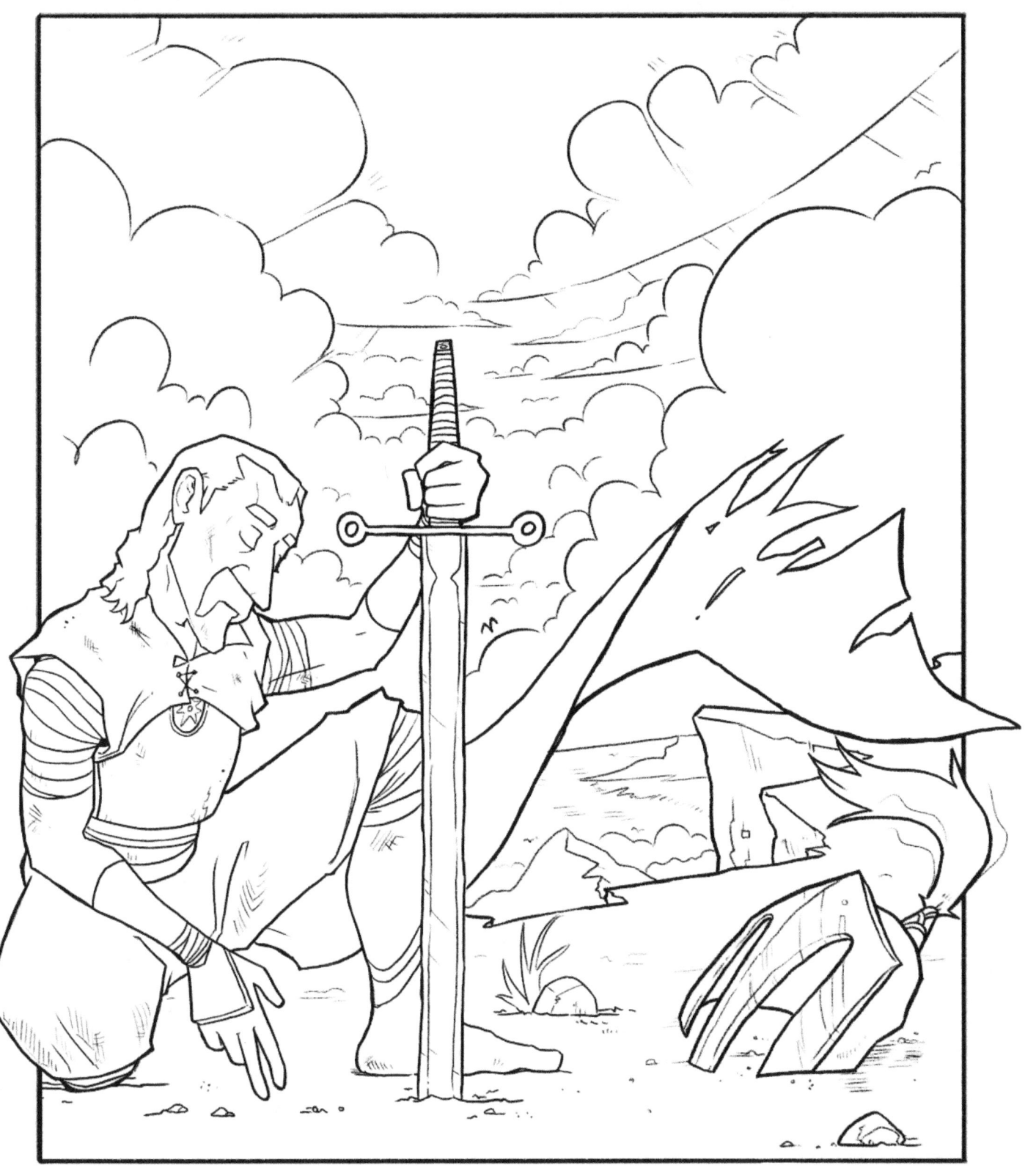

At the top of Mount Egyseg, warriors pay tribute to their fallen brethren.

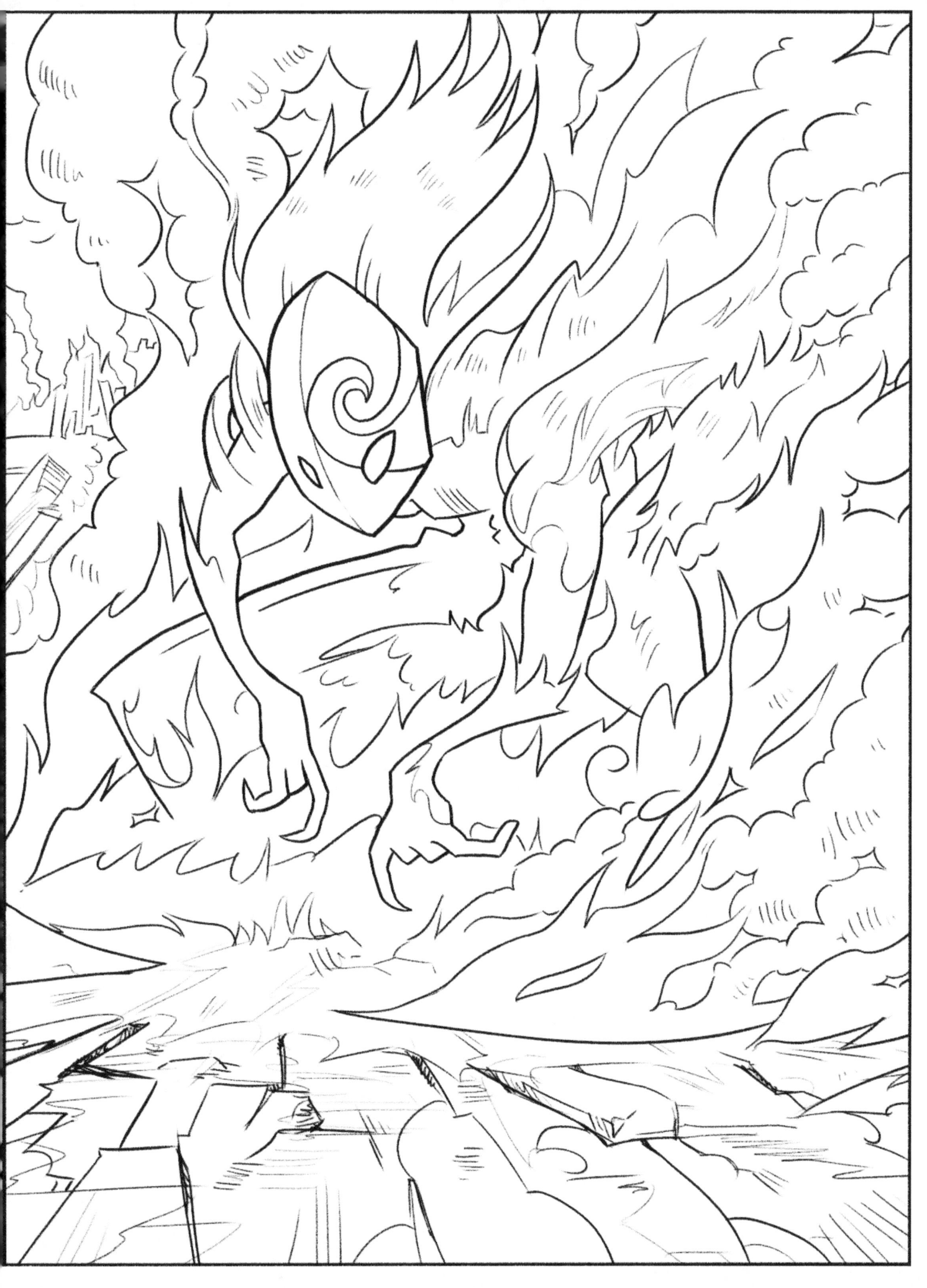

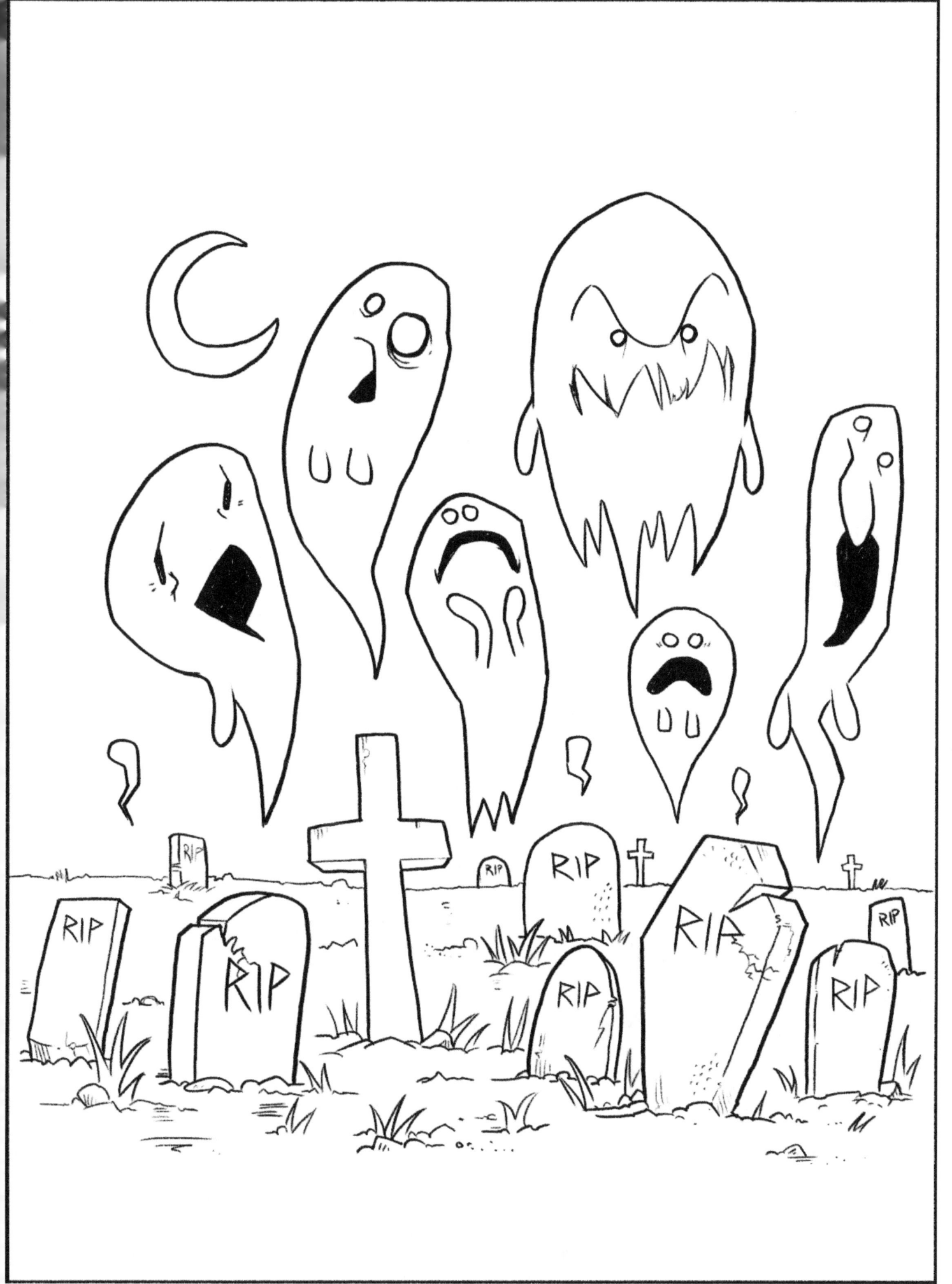

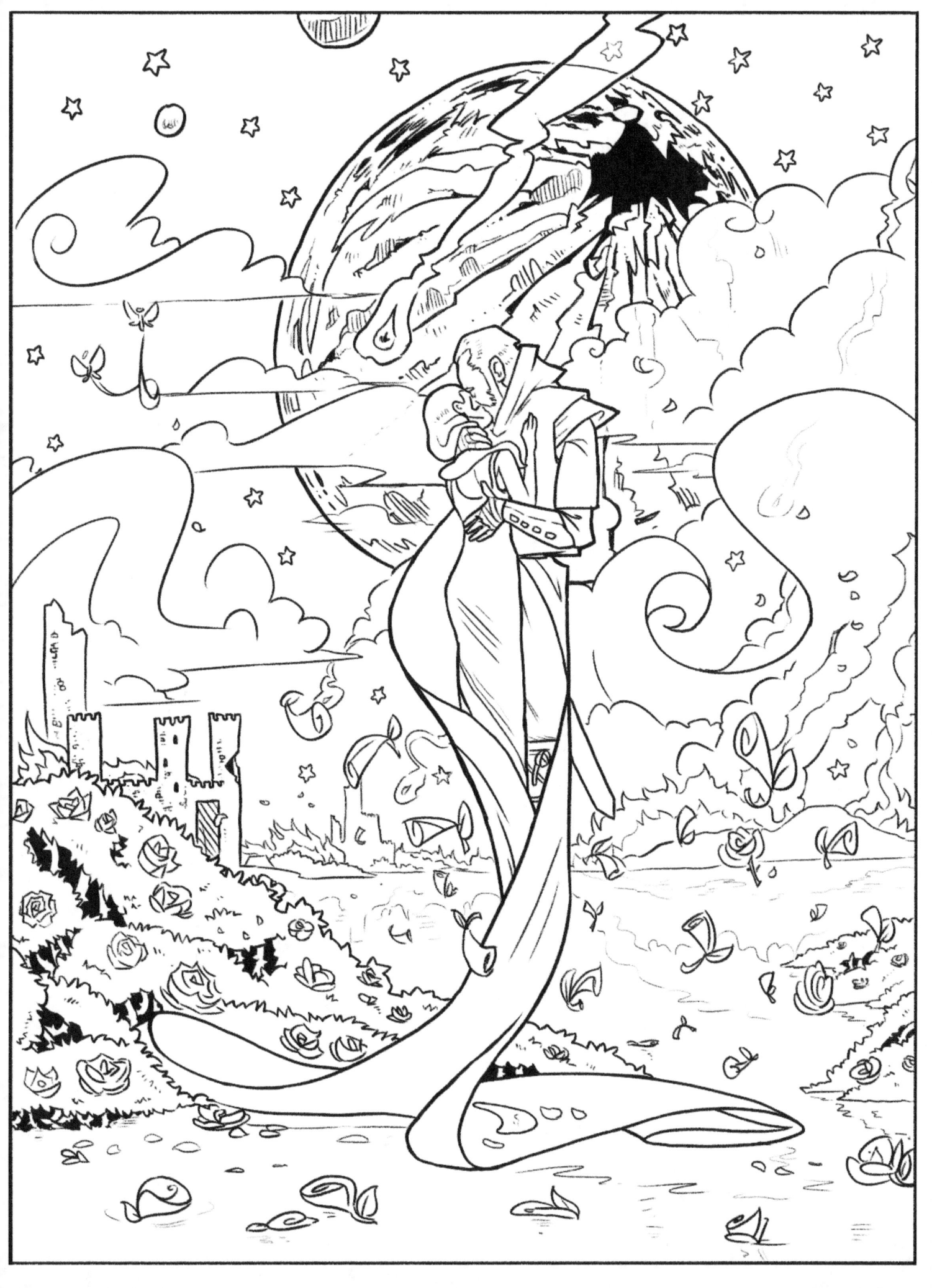

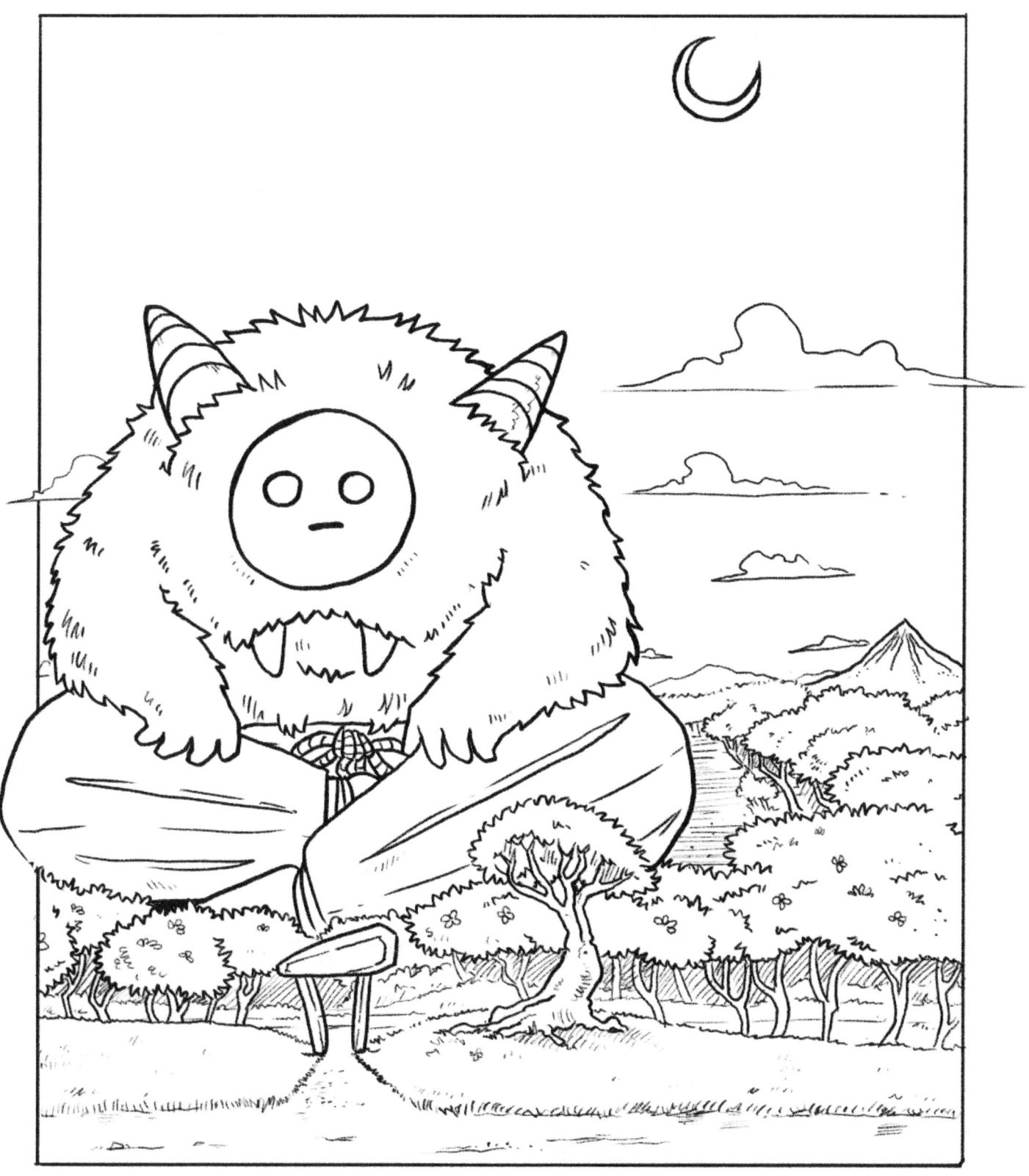

Here, the Guardian
of the Celestial Gate sits.

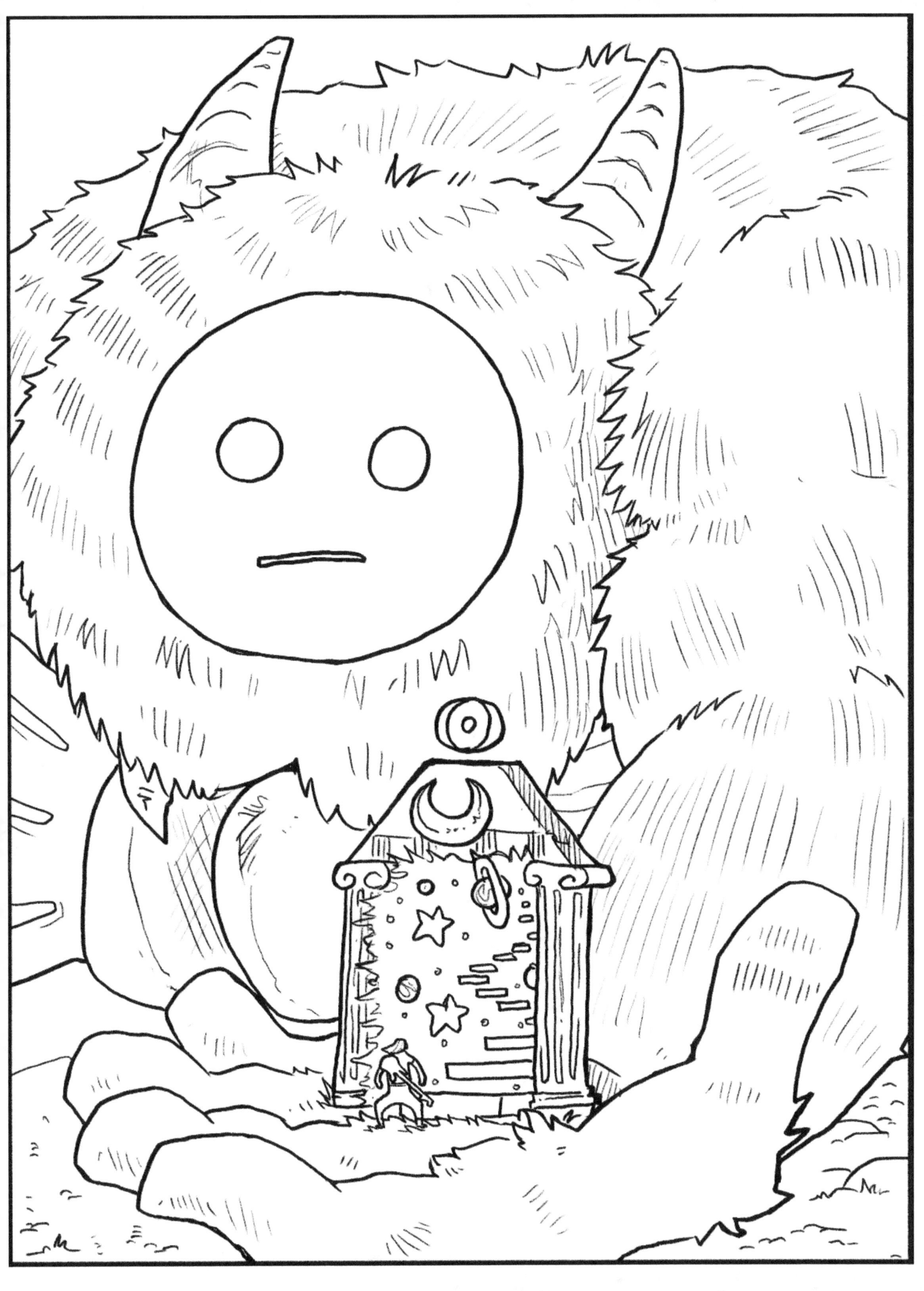

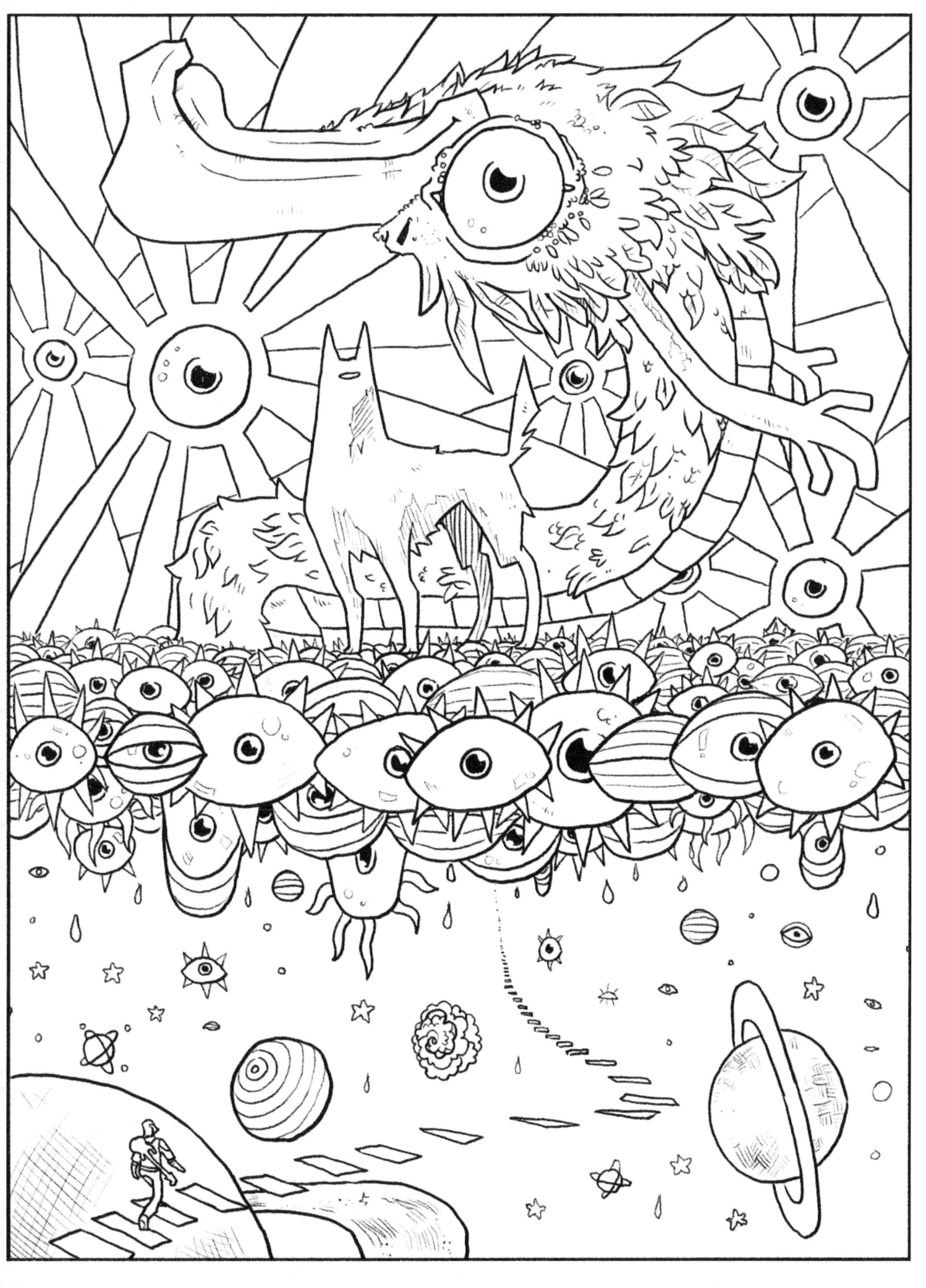

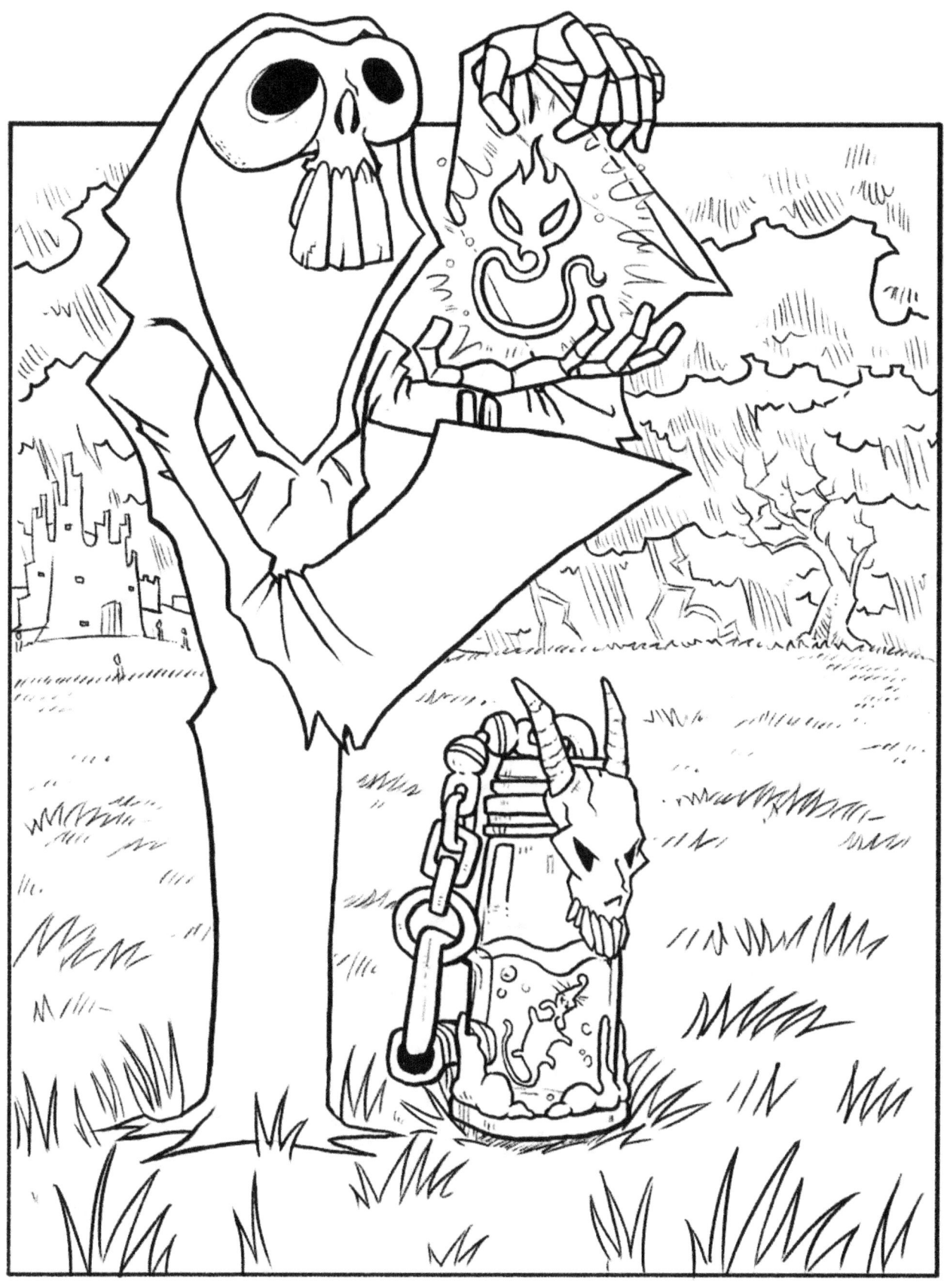

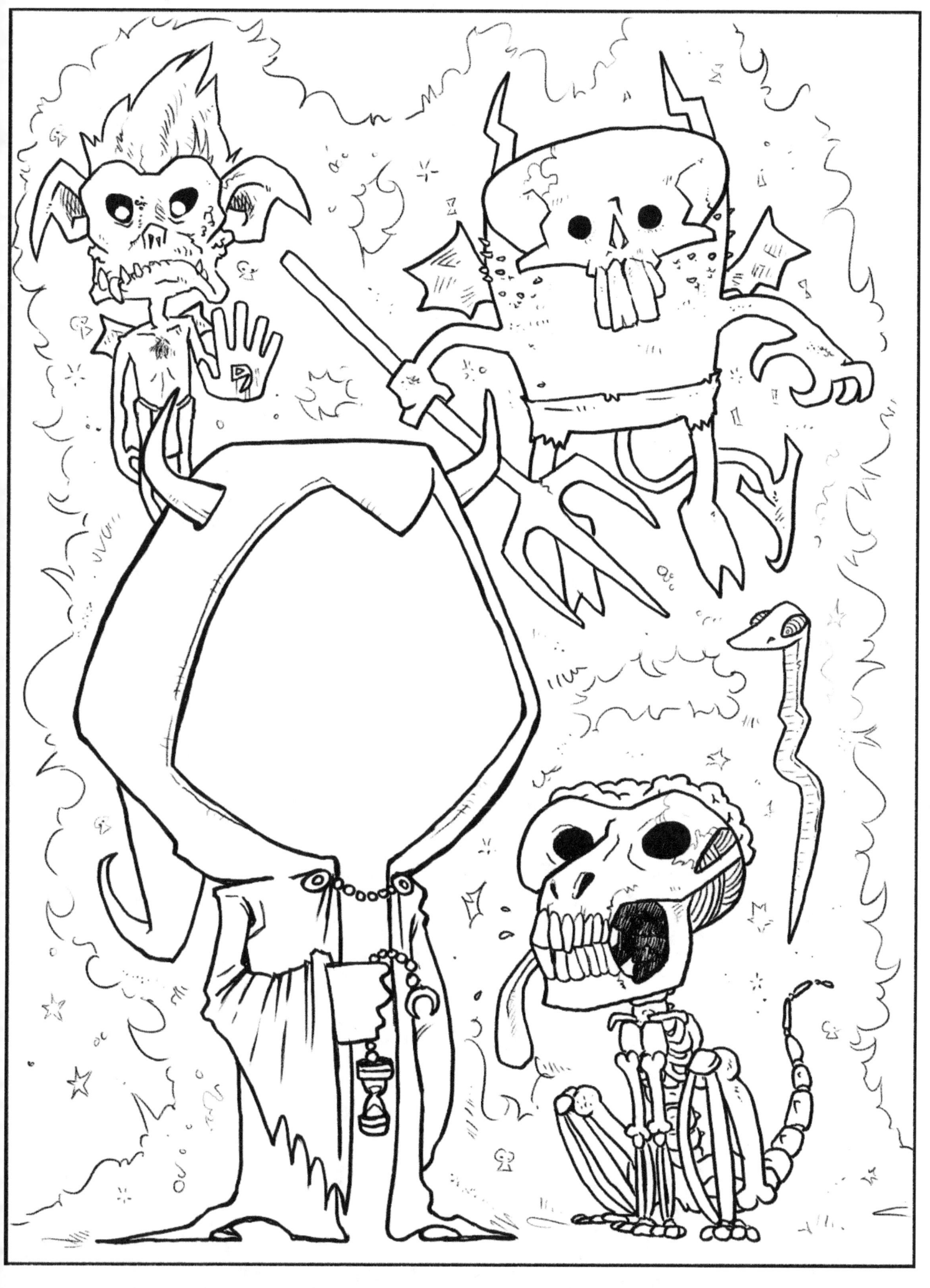

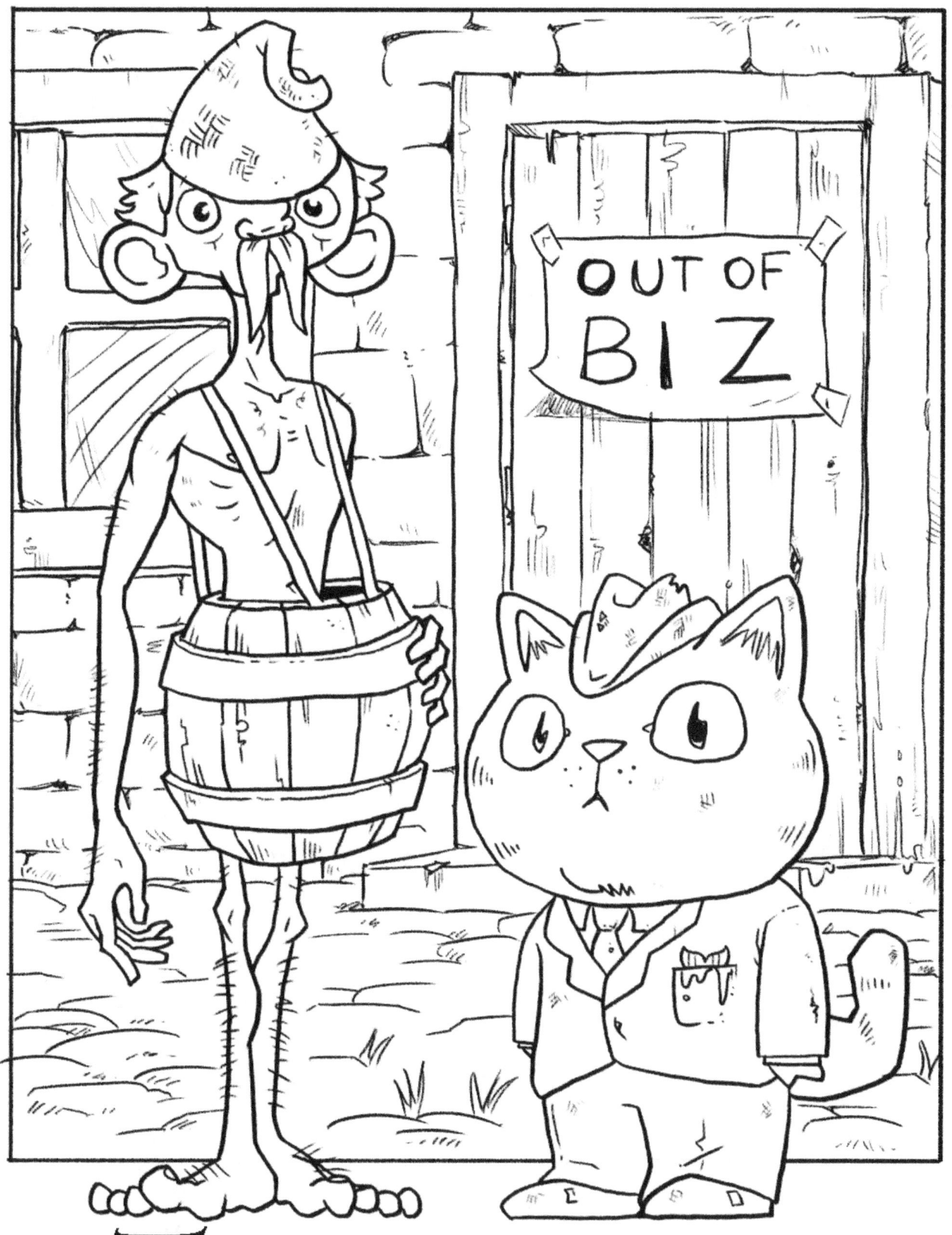

Tough times for the
Fartsburg Financial Sector

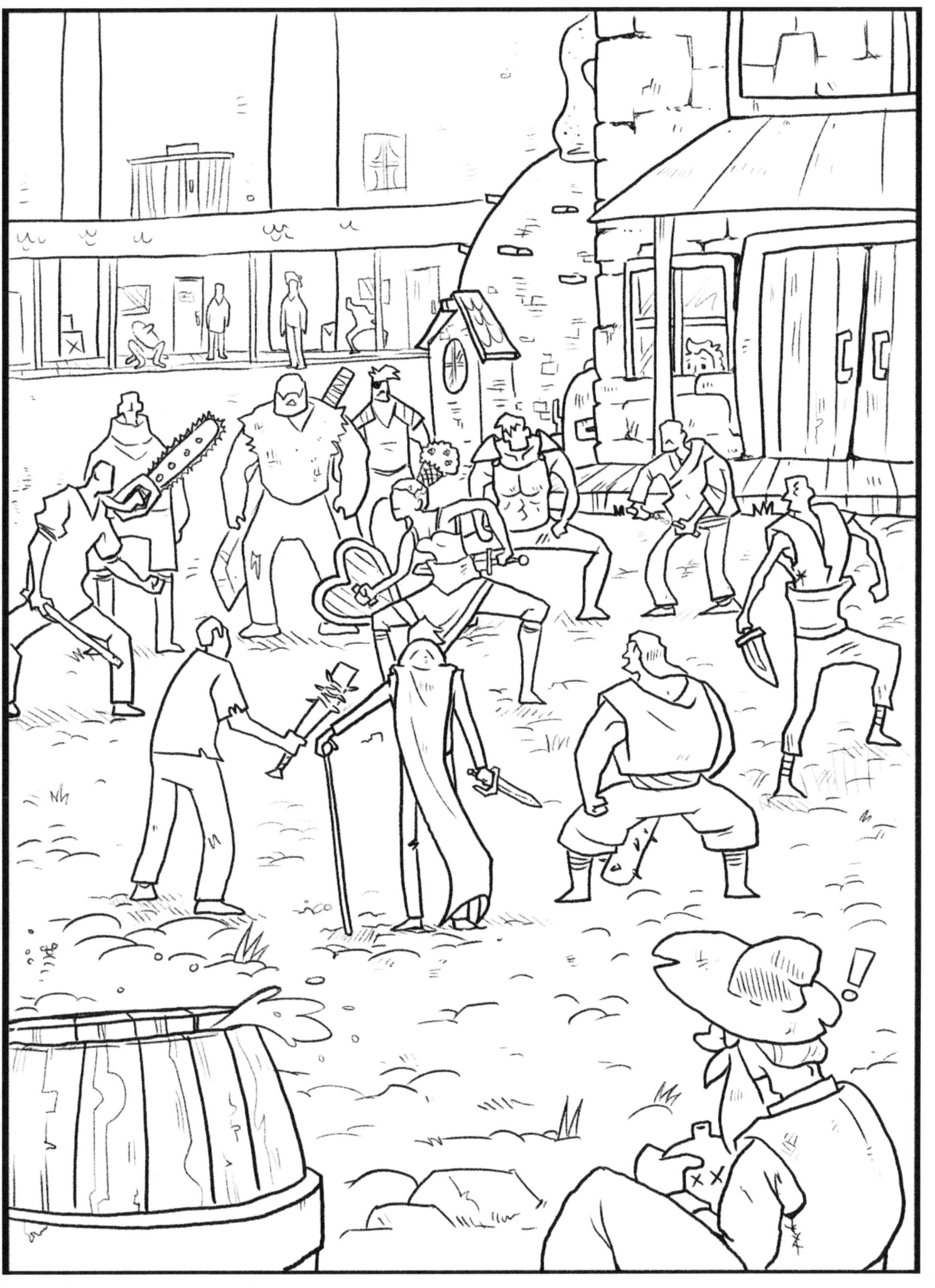

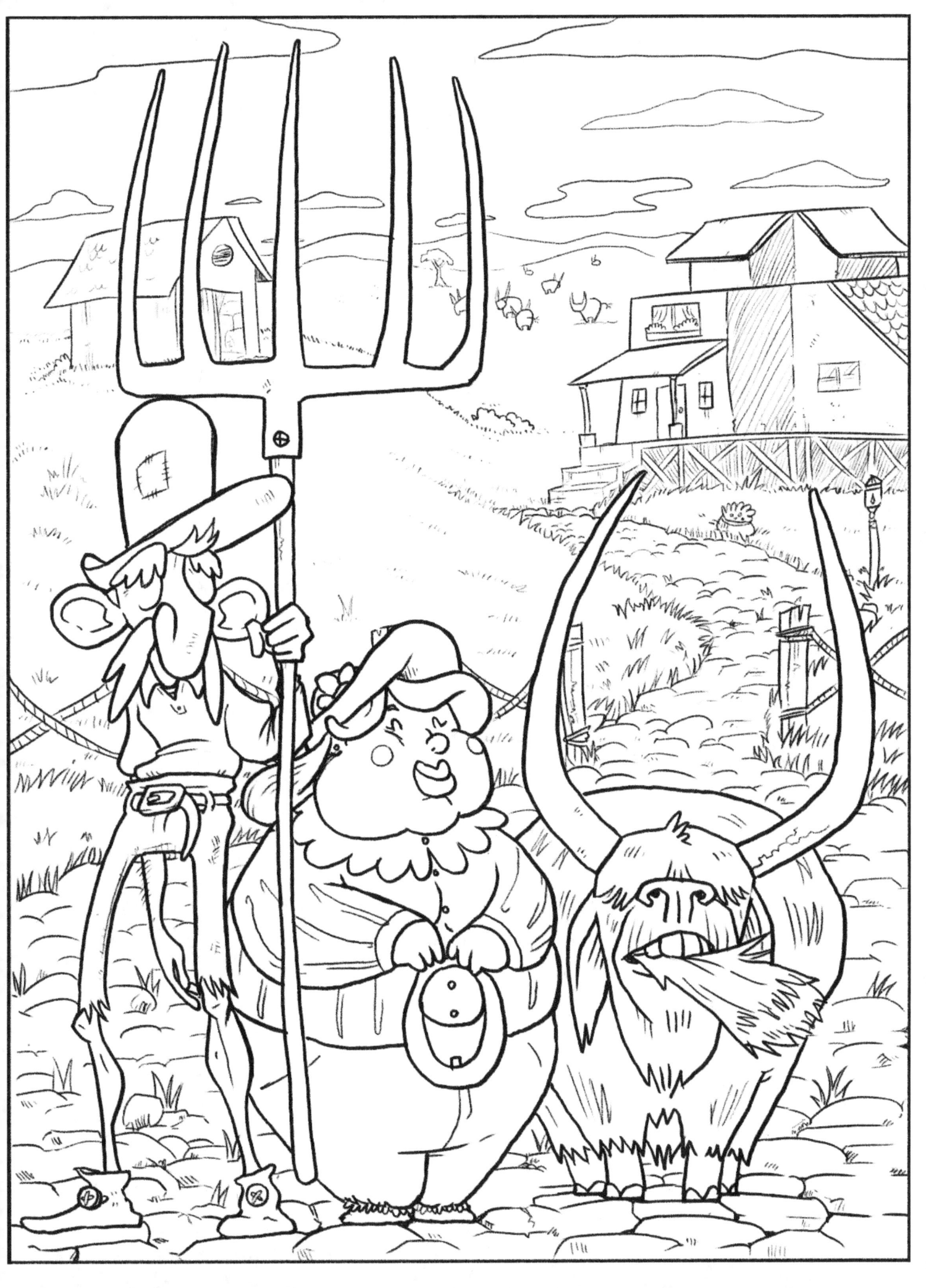

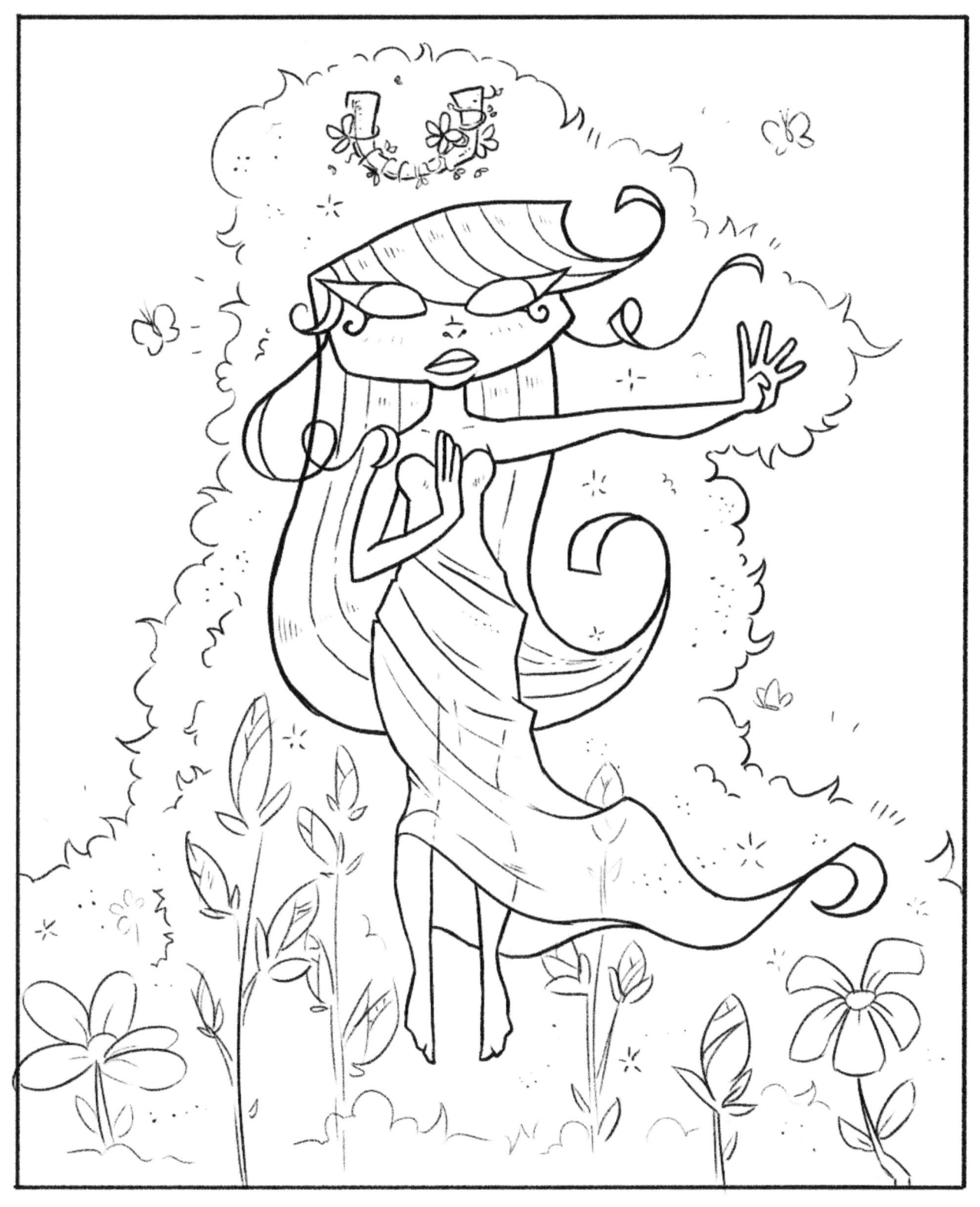

The men and women of the
Western Plains owe it all to the
Lady of the Harvest.

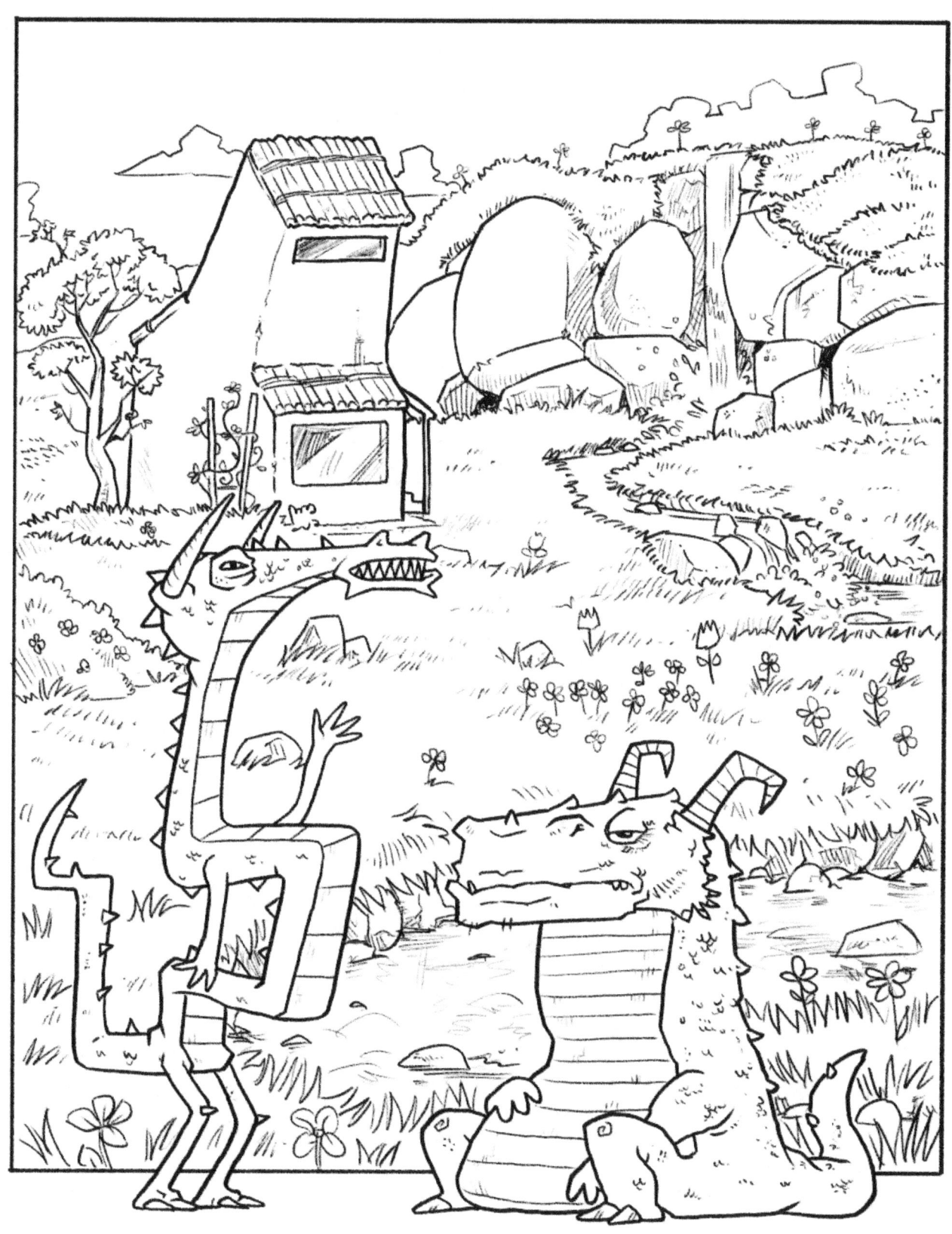

Come in! Stay a night! Rest a while!

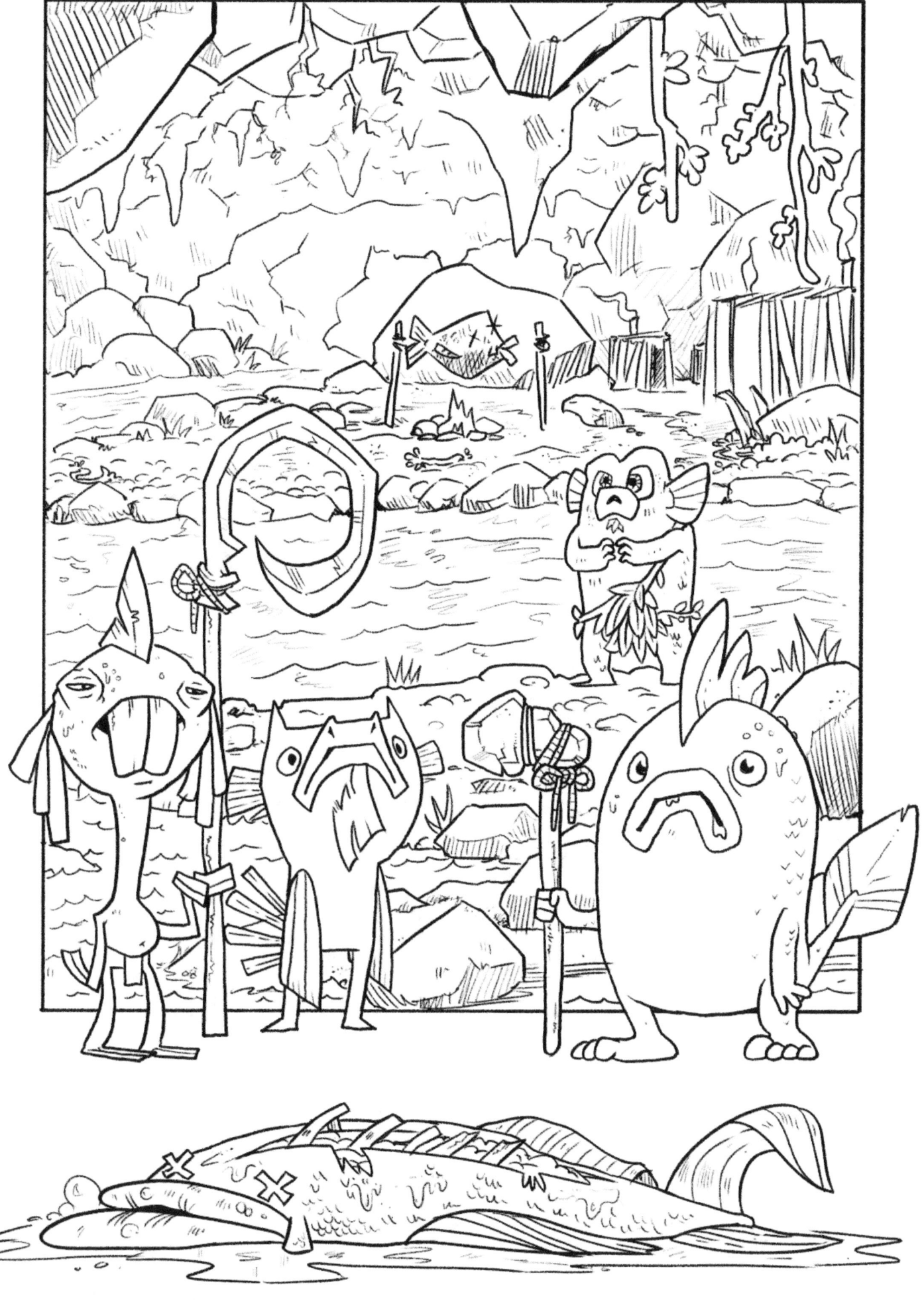

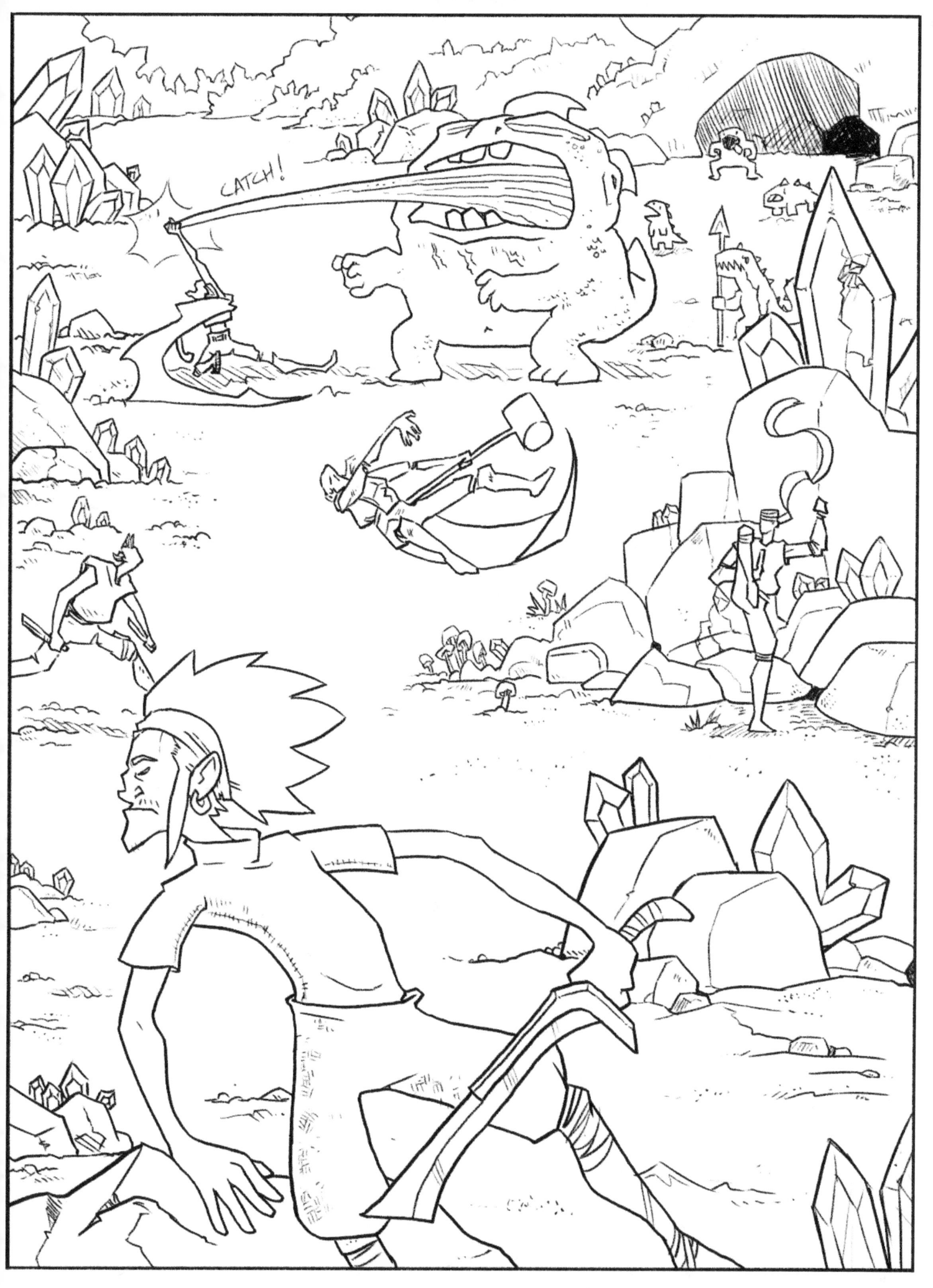

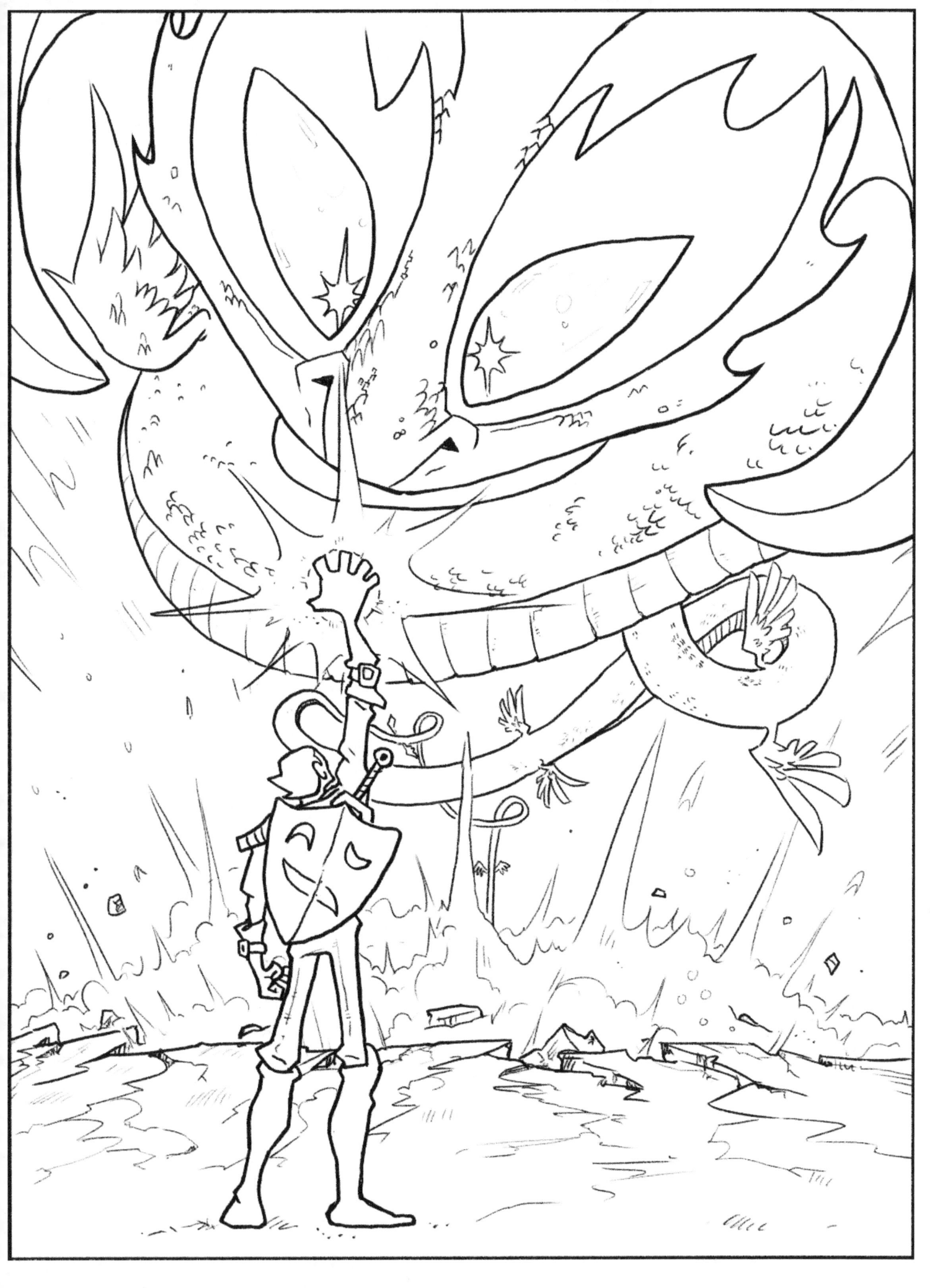

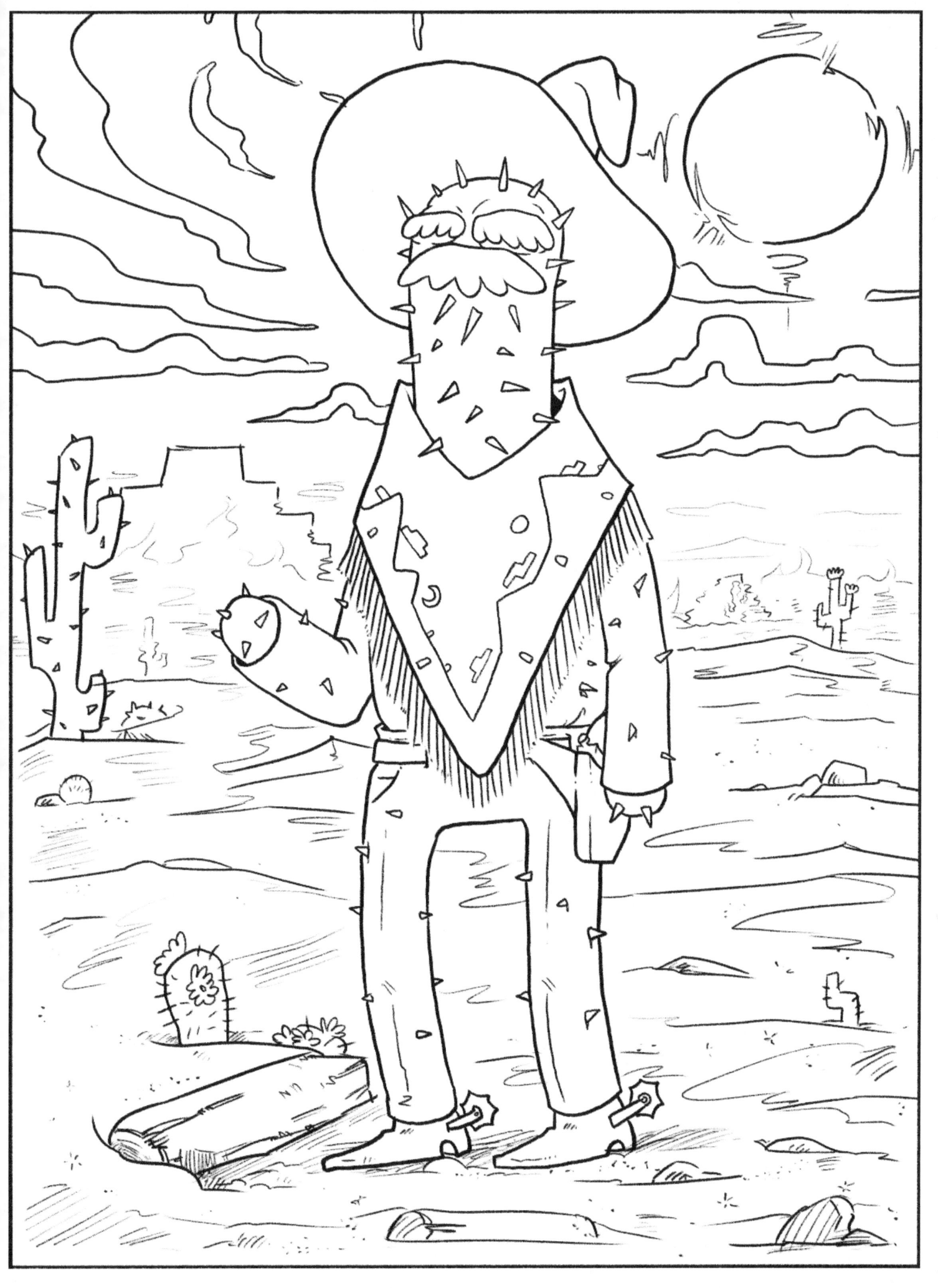

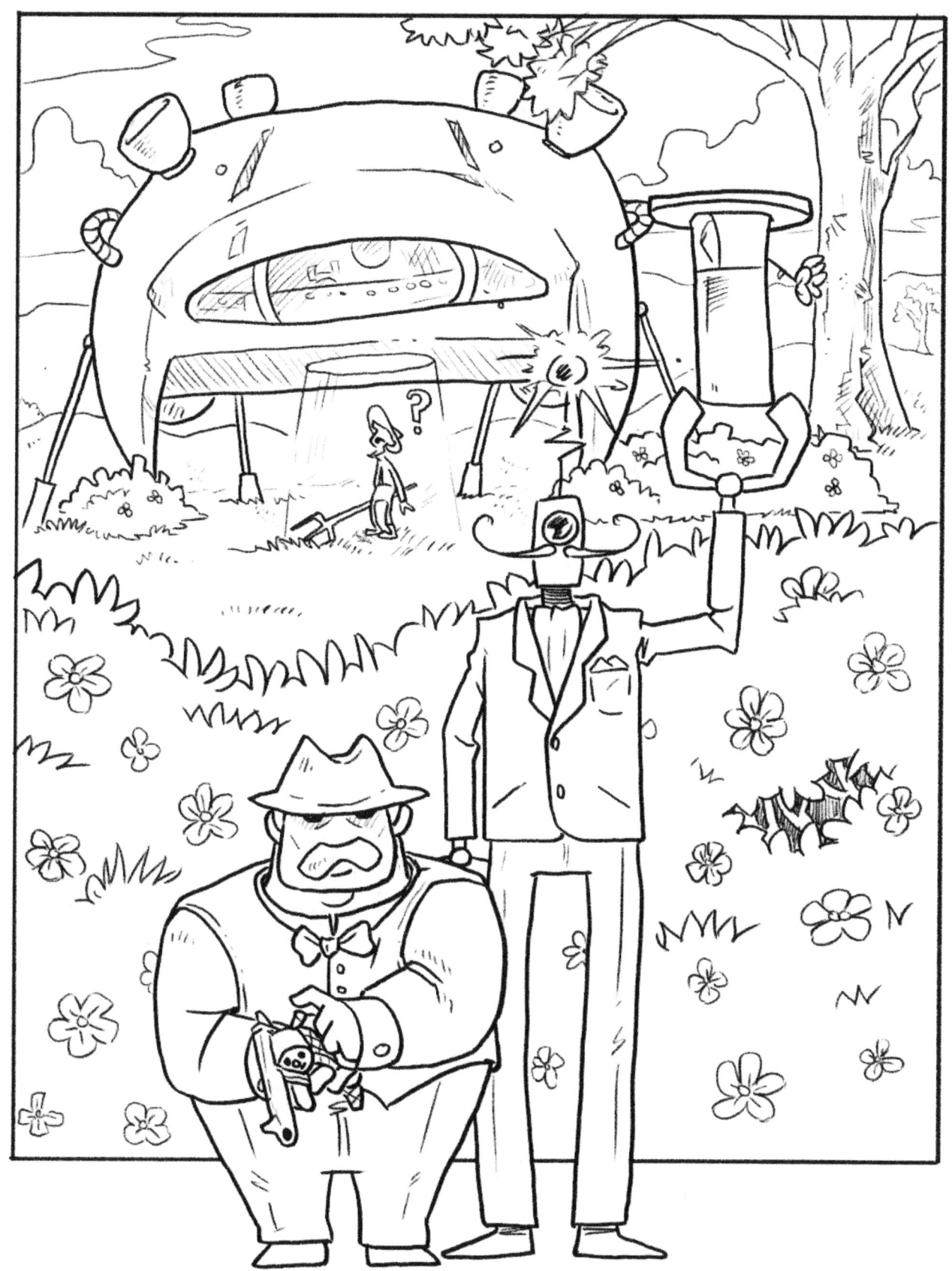

Don't Get swindled.

Thanks for enjoying my first coloring book!
Magic,Myth & Monsters Issue #1

Visit fenczikdesign.com and magicmythandmonsters.tumblr.com
for more art, music and everything Magic, Myth & Monsters.

Feel free to contact me at stevenfenczik@gmail.com

www.ingramcontent.com/pod-product-compliance
Lightning Source LLC
Chambersburg PA
CBHW081612170526
45166CB00009B/2938

9 781519 728425